Prais

"Imagine taking the whirlwind of unknowns, fears and things you want to learn about when you are starting your own business and having the answers to them available in just one place. That is what *Good to Grow* is. It is the only book you need. It's like having your own cheering squad, best friend, and sage advisor, all in one place. Laura has an uncanny ability to make the transition to entrepreneurship feel doable, attainable and with her mix of personal experience woven in, it feels like you are actually *good to grow*! I will be recommending this book to anyone starting this journey."

Catherine Farquharson | Mindset & Transformation Coach, Catherine Farquharson Coaching

"You might want to buy a new pack of highlighters with this book. It's that good. Laura completely captured the mindset roadblocks that drain our energy, the practical action items that we so easily get hung up on, and the experience of being an entrepreneur. Laura nails it with *Good to Grow* from both the mindset and functional aspects of being an entrepreneur. If you're considering taking the leap, read this book and join the club with your eyes wide open."

Michelle Tresemer | Owner, Foundations First Marketing

"*Good to Grow* both teaches and inspires. Rich in detail and full of poignant insights, this book is an indispensable introduction to entrepreneurship that guides readers through important areas for reflection. While the book is written from the point of view of a woman and mother, it provides businesses of any nature with action steps for every stage of growing a business."

Barbara Mowat | President & Founder, GroYourBiz Ltd.

"I've worked with hundreds of business owners and what I know for certain is that the biggest barrier to business growth is the business owner not having the right mindset. I highly recommend this book to business owners at all stages. Laura makes readers feel confident that they are not alone, and she gives them tools to get into the business owner's mindset. I loved the curated resources and really appreciated the exercises for self-discovery, practice, and reinforcement."

Judi Hughes | Partner, Your Planning Partners Ltd.

"The number one job of an entrepreneur is to be a creator of jobs, not the doer. As you transition from employee to entrepreneur, it will feel easier to just do all the work. But, at some point, you will discover that won't support a sustainable business. *Good to Grow* will help you to build the foundation of a healthy business...a business that runs itself."

Mike Michalowicz | Author of *Clockwork, Profit First* and *Get Different*

"As a female entrepreneur who has run my own company for 15 years, I am amazed at how much insight this book provided. When I started my entrepreneurial journey, I jumped in with both feet and learned as I went. I wish I had this book to guide me all those years ago. This book is filled with so much clever advice and insight on topics that most people don't even consider. For me it was a great 'refresh' on growing a business from the ground up."

Tiffany Richardson | Owner, Icing Marketing Corporation and Founder, Half Full Most Days

"Laura is one of the most thoughtful people I know. She is a marketing genius and has a solid understanding of the journey when moving from being an employee to owning your own business. It does not matter where you are at in your professional development/career path, this book is a must read for everyone."

Marty Britton | President & CEO, Britton Management Profiles Inc.

"Starting your own business is not for the faint of heart. It takes courage, especially if you are giving up a paid gig to branch out on your own. *Good to Grow* provides you with the tools and roadmap to navigate this journey and Laura draws on her own experiences to help you succeed. As she observes, connecting with other women who are on the same path, helps reduce the isolation you may be feeling when you embark on this new venture."

Anne Day | Founder, Company of Women

"My partners and I started Mabel's Labels because we saw a need in the market and I personally needed more flexibility in my work to allow time to support my son with autism. I wouldn't say I was a natural entrepreneur, but I always had a good mindset. I think that's one of the key reasons I was successful. This is the book I wish I had when I started out. *Good to Grow* offers so much wisdom and actionable advice that will help prepare new business owners."

Julie Cole | Co-Founder and Senior Director, Public Relations, Mabel's Labels Inc.

"Whether you're new to the entrepreneurial world, or have been around the block a few times, Laura's book is a must-read – filled with valuable information that reads like a chat with a girlfriend from someone who has experienced the journey herself and is sharing all the details. This is not a checklist of to dos, but rather a review of areas to explore, examine and evaluate – helping to strengthen your foundation with both mindset principles and business practicality."

Rosie Coelho | Owner, Rosie's Kitchen Co.

"As a recent graduate of the "life after corporate" club myself, I can unequivocally say that I wrestled with many of the questions Laura expertly brings to the surface in *Good to Grow*. Leaving the safety net of a steady paycheque is an overwhelming identity shift, much harder than the actual creation of a business. For any woman thinking of pursuing entrepreneurship, I have two pieces of advice for you: hire a coach and keep this book on your bedside table. It's an invaluable companion you will return to, time and time again."

Teresa Vozza | CEO & Founder, Teresa Vozza Coaching

"If you are an entrepreneur feeling lost or someone preparing to start a business, *Good to Grow* is a MUST. Thousands of resources exist to tell you all the steps to starting a business, but few share what has to happen first: your major mindset/identity shift that if left unaddressed will sabotage you and your business. Laura will coach you through the full picture of being a business owner, through both the practical side and the internal side and how they intertwine."

Adeline Hull | Owner, Elevated Edit

"This book is a must read for all budding entrepreneurs. It is chock full of wisdom, insights, personal stories, and quotes from Laura and other successful business owners. Laura has masterfully distilled a wealth of knowledge into an enjoyable read. You will come away with a collection of practical takeaways to create a thriving business."

Alison Cruise | Owner, Sadhana Yoga

"Laura perfectly nailed it with *Good to Grow*. It highlights so many critical lessons for entrepreneurs, both for those just starting out as well as the seasoned. I love the focus on aligning your values with your business. To approach business any other way will leave you missing a vital component to reach success and happiness. This should be required reading for anyone who calls themselves an entrepreneur. I wish I had this book 15 years ago when I left the corporate world."

Jodie Pappas | Owner, Clean Kiss

"A must read for anyone contemplating the shift from employment to entrepreneurship. And a step-by-step guide for business owners striving to achieve balance in life, as well as excellence in business."

Margaret Hachey | Managing Director, Ontario & Eastern Canada, GroYourBiz Ltd.

good to grow

Cultivate Your Mindset and Habits to Thrive as an Entrepreneur

LAURA VALVASORI

Hasmark Publishing
www.hasmarkpublishing.com

Disclaimer

This book is designed to provide information and motivation to our readers. It is sold with the understanding that the publisher is not engaged to render any type of psychological, legal, or any other kind of professional advice. The content of each article is the sole expression and opinion of its author, and not necessarily that of the publisher. No warranties or guarantees are expressed or implied by the publisher's choice to include any of the content in this volume. Neither the publisher nor the individual author(s) shall be liable for any physical, psychological, emotional, financial, or commercial damages, including, but not limited to, special, incidental, consequential or other damages. Our views and rights are the same: You are responsible for your own choices, actions, and results.

Permission should be addressed in writing to Laura Valvasori at laura@goodtogrowmarketing.ca

Editors: Adeline Hull, Brad Green
Cover Design: Anne Karklins anne@hasmarkpublishing.com
Cover Image: Kemal Christian Catovic from pexels.com
Interior Layout: Anne Karklins anne@hasmarkpublishing.com

ISBN 13: 978-1-77482-170-1
ISBN 10: 1774821702

For Stella and Gavin.
May you always know that you can create
your own reality, carve your own path,
and build a life you love.

Table of Contents

Preface

"When you look at successful women, they have other women who have supported them, and they've gotten to where they are because of those women."

— Sheryl Sandberg

I SPENT FIFTEEN YEARS IN THE CORPORATE WORLD. For many of those years, I had a nagging feeling that something was missing. Eventually, I decided to listen to the whispers of my soul and take the leap into entrepreneurship. Since making that decision, I've created a successful consulting business and a life I love. My vision for this book is to inspire and empower you to thrive as an entrepreneur and create a life *you* love!

I have learned a lot about running a business—and about myself. I've expanded from my corporate roots and developed a vast network of fellow entrepreneurs. Having lived in both worlds, I now understand the nuances of how being an employee impacts your way of living and everyday existence; how it creates deeply ingrained beliefs and habits. I have also experienced the challenges and blessings of entrepreneurship.

When I embarked on the path of self-employment, I had little understanding of just how much I would need to change my habitual way of thinking and operating to shift from employee to business owner and entrepreneur. I also didn't understand how many new self and business management skills I would be required to learn.

Many entrepreneurs struggle to adjust to their new role and identity. There are many books about the business side of starting a business: How to make a business plan; how to register your business; how to create a marketing plan, and on and on. However, I haven't come across many books that talk about what you, as a person, will experience, or the new realities you'll face. This is an important topic that needs to be discussed more openly among those who have made the choice to leave traditional employment to start a business, or those who are in the early stages of self-employment.

The personal transformation can be a bit like moving from grade school to high school. There is no longer anyone holding your hand and giving you detailed directions. You have newfound freedom, but with it comes a new level of personal responsibility. You are now in charge of your own world in a way that you may have never been before, and you need to tend to and manage your internal world in new ways.

As a business owner, *you* must always continue to grow as a person. You are the heart and soul of your business, and your business is an expression of you! When you become intentional about the business you are creating, and develop the right mindset and habits, you set yourself up to become a thriving entrepreneur. As an extension of your personal thriving, you will be able to build a business that thrives as well.

The process is like a farmer preparing their soil for planting. Rather than land, you are cultivating the mindset and habits that will create the fertile soil where the seeds of your business will be planted.

Preparing for a New You

Regardless of the type of business you plan to create, there are things you'll have to do when starting out. These include developing your brand, defining your target market, creating your offerings, and attracting clients.

Outside of these tasks, there is also an internal emotional journey that takes place. The more you are aware of and prepare yourself for what lies ahead, the more seamlessly you'll shift into entrepreneurship.

Doesn't "thriving" sound so much better than "burning out" in the process of building a business?

So, what do I mean by thriving? Thriving means feeling fulfilled by your work. Thriving means spending more time doing what you love and being of the most service. Thriving means stretching beyond your limits and growing. Thriving means attracting amazing clients and having income flowing in. And lastly, thriving means finding joy in your daily life, and feeling mentally, physically, and spiritually healthy.

We will further explore what thriving means to you.

Don't Jump into Taking Action

When coming out of the corporate world or traditional employment, our natural inclination is to jump into taking action. That is what we have been programmed to do and are rewarded for. It is a learned habit: make the plan, and rush into executing it.

Yes, developing your marketing plan and creating a website are important steps, and necessary! However, if you don't also make the necessary shifts internally, your ability to take effective action may be limited.

Taking action with the right energy, rooted in the right mindset, and supported by the right habits is the game-changer.

I've learned through my own experience, and through working with clients, that we often think we need more business knowledge, or that we must do more to solve the problems that come up in our business. The truth is that mindset—not skill set— is often the root of the problem. We are the only ones impeding ourselves from moving forward.

There are enough challenges to overcome in starting a business without making it more difficult for yourself. I once walked by a coffee shop that had a message board out front that was as true as it was funny. It read, "I've got ninety-nine problems and eighty-six of them are completely made-up scenarios in my head that I'm stressing out about for absolutely no reason."

Many successful entrepreneurs come to a point, usually several years into their business, where they realize the power of their mindset. They begin to understand that the more they learn to work with their mindset and grow on a personal level, the more successful their business will become.

There are many examples of highly successful people that are advocates of studying mindset. One of these people is Sara Blakely, the founder of Spanx and youngest self-made female billionaire in the world. Sara shared in an Instagram post that she found mindset after going through a tragedy at the age of sixteen. It was then that she began listening to Dr. Wayne Dyer. The post read:

> "I realized I could teach myself how to think. Major epiphany. How to think in a way that would propel me forward not hold me back. Think in a way that could silence the negative voices in my head. Think in a way that allowed me to look for the good in everything bad. Think in a way that made me believe I could manifest and visualize the life I wanted into existence (with a ton

of hard work.) It takes a lot of practice and repetition. It's like a muscle. You can have all the talent and genius in the world but if you haven't trained your mind to think optimally, it's often wasted. I'm still a student of mindset…always will be."

This book will help you develop the knowledge and practices that will accelerate your personal growth so that you don't have to wait years to figure it out for yourself.

The Power of Your Mindset

You don't know what you don't know, and that was certainly the case for me. I didn't understand until recently how powerful our minds are, and that our experiences in life are dictated by our mindset.

In the early years of my business, my internal experience was tumultuous. On the outside I was successful, but on the inside, I was putting a tremendous amount of pressure on myself. I tried to force and control achieving my goals through grit and will. I was always worried about one thing or another and didn't allow myself to enjoy life. I can now see that some health challenges I was experiencing during that time were my body trying to tell me that there is a better way.

I've always been interested in personal development. I spent years reading books and taking courses, but I always felt like something was missing. Then I discovered mindset work, and everything changed. Over the past several years, I've become a dedicated student of mindset. I hired my own coach and have been studying leaders in the field including Bob Proctor, Abraham-Hicks, Mel Robbins, and other authors such as Wallace Wattles, Neville Goddard, and Thomas Troward. I am a part of a community of women that live and breathe mindset-related material every day.

A common misunderstanding is that mindset is simply about positive thinking. However, mindset is really about developing an understanding of how the thoughts you repeatedly think—and the beliefs you hold—shape the lens through which you see the world and yourself. It is about understanding the personal power you have in creating your own reality. Your mindset influences how you think, feel, and behave in any situation, including in the creation of your business.

Through my time studying mindset, I've experienced profound changes in my life. I now have awareness and tools I wish I had applied in my business from day one. This has changed my internal experience and helped me to be more confident. It has changed how I show up more authentically in my business. Doing mindset work has helped me to see my own potential and step into my personal power. Today I am a happier person who enjoys my life more than I ever have before.

I've gone from being a very logical and analytical person to taking a more spiritually connected approach to my life and business practices. I have a more relaxed attitude, and now intentionally use my thoughts to my benefit. I care about how I feel, rather than just focusing on achievement at the expense of my mental and physical health. I understand how energy relates to all aspects of my life, and I tap into my intuition to help guide me.

My mindset study has also had an impact on my family. By witnessing me and being open to some of the tools I share, my children are absorbing these ideas and are creating a strong foundation for themselves as individuals. It is normalized in our home to talk about managing our thoughts and energy. My teenage son Gavin was just telling me last night that he has started taking cold showers as an exercise to train his mind to control his thinking. All I could do was smile.

As I have shared with my family and friends, I am now excited to share some of what I've learned with you.

Success Starts with Habits

In *Atomic Habits: An Easy & Proven Way to Build Good Habits & Break Bad Ones* by James Clear, the author shares, "It is so easy to overestimate the importance of a defining moment and underestimate the value of making small improvements daily. Too often, we convince ourselves that massive success requires massive action."

The systems you put in place, the habitual way you approach things, and the small habits you establish will help bring the most effective version of yourself to your business.

When you combine mindset with habits, you have a recipe for success.

Why Many Are Taking the Leap

There are many things happening around the world that are affecting the way people think when it comes to work. Trends are indicating that more people are considering entrepreneurship in the coming years. I feel this trend in my own life with the number of people who reach out to me asking to pick my brain about my experience as an entrepreneur. They share with me that they want more flexibility and control over their time. They are done with long commutes, or with making sacrifices to their health. They wish to work for companies that will support them and that align with their values, or they want to build their own businesses.

The global pandemic created a collective wake-up call, and many people do not want to return to the corporate world or a traditional employment model. They have reflected on their career and lifestyle choices and have become reconnected to the things that matter most to them. They have had the great realization that they want more from their lives than what traditional employment can offer.

Many people are choosing to leave the corporate world to start businesses that allow them to pursue meaningful careers and have more freedom over their working experience. The saying "life is too short" has never been more burned into people's minds than after living through the pandemic.

A large percentage of those people who are choosing to start their own businesses are women. Women are wanting more flexibility in owning their time and are motivated by the idea of making an impact.

In *Sacred Success* by Barbara Stanny, the author references a study conducted by the Simmons School of Management which found that 70% of women polled reported they were driven not by "perks, position, or personal gain," but by "a desire to help others, contribute to communities, and make the world a better place."

There is also a trend in the workforce where smaller or scaling businesses are hiring "fractional executives." This is a practice of hiring people for a lesser time commitment in areas such as marketing, finance, and operations, allowing the company to access senior skills at a more reasonable investment than a full-time role would require. This provides an incredible opportunity for those with specific expertise to start knowledge-based businesses.

I'm very excited by the increasing number of women stepping into roles as business owners. In Canada, only 17% of Canadian[1] small and medium-sized businesses are owned by women. Studies

[1] https://ised-isde.canada.ca/site/women-entrepreneurship-strategy/en

---

Note: Throughout the book, I've used the terms entrepreneur, business owner, freelancer, or being self-employed interchangeably. Everyone identifies with a different term so please substitute whichever you prefer! I've also used the term women to refer to all individuals who identify as women.

show that by advancing gender equality and the participation of women in the economy, Canada could add up to $150 billion in GDP. With those statistics representing only Canada, imagine the impact that increasing female entrepreneurship could have around the world!

It breaks my heart when I meet a woman that has something incredible to offer, but who is missing the bit of direction or support she needs to bring her gifts to the world. If reading this book helps just one woman gain knowledge that will enable her to be successful, then I will have achieved my goal of using my experience to support and empower other women.

What Can You Expect from this Book?

My goal is to prepare you for your new experience and give you the tools to set yourself up for successful entrepreneurship. By adopting the right approach early on, you will be "good to grow" into your new role.

I understand how lonely and overwhelming it can feel when starting out on your own. I want you to think of this book as a pocket mentor for your journey. It will equip you with knowledge and guidance to help you along the way, and it can always be referred to in times of doubt.

A good friend told me that she often hears my voice in her head when she's facing a challenge in her business. She hears me asking questions like, "Are you giving energy to focusing on what you want to happen right now?" or "What are you believing to be true?" She said these questions shake her out of the moment when she is feeling stuck. In the same way, I would love it if what you learn from this book comes back to you when you need it the most.

Throughout this book, you'll be introduced to insights distilled from my experience and study that relate specifically to being a business owner. I've shared best practices, advice, and habits to apply to key areas of your business. I've also included quotes and stories from some of the over thirty thriving women entrepreneurs who shared their wisdom for this book. By learning from those who have gone before, you'll save time and money, and most certainly a few tears.

I would like to acknowledge that I've written this book from my perspective and experience based on who I am—a woman living in Canada, a wife, and a mother. I've included some topics that will resonate more specifically with women, but the majority of this book's content will be equally relevant, and I hope helpful, for people of all genders.

As an avid reader, I have acquired a wealth of knowledge I would love to share with you. I've referenced several books to further accelerate your learning. If you want to dive even deeper, you can refer to the Works Cited and Resources section at the end of the book.

I've also included a blank page at the end of each chapter for you to answer two questions: "What were your key takeaways from this chapter?" and "What new ideas will you commit to trying or implementing in your business?" Knowing that you'll be asked to answer these questions at the end of each chapter will help focus your mind on finding the answers as you read.

By the end of *Good to Grow*, you will feel empowered in your role as a business owner. You will be ready to grow into a thriving entrepreneur and build a successful business and life you love.

Before we take our first practical steps, I would like to share a bit about who I am and how my road to entrepreneurship unfolded. You might recognize some of your own story in mine.

My Bumpy Road
to Entrepreneurship

AFTER COMPLETING A DEGREE IN MARKETING, I began to work for a small accounting firm, and then moved on to work for a law firm. A few years later I married my long-time boyfriend and best friend, and we had two children. Like so many other women trying to commute, build a career, and manage a young family, I struggled.

Even though I was extremely fortunate to have a bit of flexibility, a supportive husband, and a close group of friends, it was still not easy. Deadlines, endless commutes, and children that could go from fine one minute to throwing up in the next meant life was always a rush. I always felt like the chaos of everyday life never quite allowed me to do anything as well as I would have liked to.

As I progressed through my career, I began to have a sense of uneasiness. These feelings grew stronger when I returned to work after having my second child. If I was going to leave my children in daycare and commute into the city, I wanted to feel like my work was making a difference in some meaningful way. I wanted to feel excited and proud.

I began to develop the feeling that there was something more out there for me, but I couldn't put my finger on exactly what that was. The tension mounting inside me was growing stronger. I was excelling and being acknowledged for my achievements, but inside I felt my level of commitment to my job waning. The politics of corporate life were extremely frustrating and draining for me. I also wanted more autonomy and flexibility around my workday than my current firm provided. I hated the amount of value that was placed on having your bum in a seat during set office hours.

Does any of this sound familiar?

BUSINESS INSIGHT

What's Driving Women to Entrepreneurship?

Let me start by saying that there are many amazing companies that provide a great working experience for their employees. And likewise, many people are happy in their corporate roles and feel supported. While many workplaces have made massive strides in being more inclusive and supportive, there are also women who still feel unsupported for various reasons.

In my research for this book, I surveyed or interviewed over thirty women who have left traditional or corporate employment to start their own businesses. When asked the question, "What wasn't working for you in your corporate career, and how did it make you feel?" I recognized common themes in the answers. These themes revolved mostly around feeling undervalued, not having autonomy over their schedule and work, frustration with the traditional hierarchal structure, not being able to do impactful work, and a desire for more balance in their lives.

Here are a few excerpts from the answers these amazing women shared:

"I always felt like a square peg in a round hole."

"Face time, politics, not feeling valued. I had enough of it."

"The more I climbed the ranks, the more I was surrounded by colleagues and executive leaders more interested in political maneuvering and more prone to tantrums. It became far less about doing great work and making material imprints on the organization. It just wasn't fun anymore."

"I had no control over my hours, my days off, my salary...it was frustrating."

"I had one too many professional development requests turned down, and I decided that if I were to grow in my career, I would need to leave."

"Two things were stressing my system: one was that I was not in alignment with my core values and my purpose in my legal career; the second was the culture, particularly as it impacted me once I became a mother. The lack of autonomy and the bias combined with the general lack of creativity in how we work, manage, and engage people at work all led me to leave."

"I reached a point where there was no more room for me to grow within the company. I kept applying for jobs in higher positions, and they kept choosing men over me. The frustrating part was that my record was year-over-year better than the men chosen for the roles. I felt completely unseen and unappreciated."

"The work wasn't satisfying anymore. The culture was becoming discouraging to be part of, and I didn't trust some of the members of the management team."

"I dreaded going to work, with the feeling of gloom starting early on Sundays. It was hard to feel engaged in my work while trying to boost my team's morale through all of it."

"I felt a lack of respect in what was a very male-dominated industry. As I became more senior, the jockeying for position only got worse. Having other people take credit for the work I had done became the norm."

"It didn't fit my personal values any longer when my kids were little, especially working with team members who were not family-centric, and who demanded that I be on call 24/7 in case they had a so-called 'HR emergency.'"

I remember one of my own particularly low points. My daughter was ill, so I gave her Advil in the daycare parking lot. I had what I thought was an important meeting that day, so I was trying to hold off her fever for long enough to make it through the meeting and get back to her. My husband was out of town, and I felt completely stuck. It is moments like these that make you question the path you're taking, wondering if the sacrifices you are making are worth it.

The reality is that in that moment, I couldn't see another way. I thought following the typical career path was what everyone did. I did not have a view of any other path. All of my friends were in corporate jobs. I didn't know any women who were entrepreneurs, and I didn't have role models to turn to as evidence for what was possible.

I eventually left the law firm to take a marketing role with a global accounting firm. I was offered a position focused on marketing to private companies, and I felt excited about the idea of supporting family businesses.

A Victim of My Own Success

At the beginning, I loved my new job. I was one of those annoying people who walked around raving about how great my job was.

I was working with a small team that operated in a very entrepreneurial way within the larger firm, and I was fired up in my new role.

I was later recognized for my leadership skills and promoted to a new role with greater responsibility and a larger team. I moved from a very autonomous role to one with greater visibility. I was thrown into the deep end of navigating the politics of a large firm.

While there were aspects of the position that I enjoyed and learned from, I still felt like I was moving further away from what I was good at and what felt rewarding for me. I also couldn't be my authentic self and was instead being coached and molded into becoming a firm-defined "leader."

I spent most of my days rushing between meetings and managing challenges with team members. As someone who loves to roll my sleeves up and tackle a project, I felt like my talents were being wasted. Each day seemed to blur into the next. I went to work every day with a knot in my stomach. I remember walking to the office playing happy songs through my headphones, doing whatever it took to psych myself up—but it never helped. I was truly unhappy.

There was one aspect of the job where I did, in fact, thrive: getting to know CEOs of successful private companies. These leaders would often come to me with questions about their marketing strategies. They wanted to know where they should be focusing, or how they could execute more effectively. In many cases, they had either a very junior marketer in their company or no in-house marketing role at all.

I started to see that what they needed was a big-picture plan for what they were trying to achieve as a business, and how to focus their marketing to reach their goals. Something started to stir inside of me. What if I could work with these companies independently to help them with their overall strategy and planning? It was only a whisper at first, but the whisper began to grow louder and louder.

I began contemplating leaving the firm to set up my own business to provide marketing strategy consulting, but I was terrified. I would lay awake at night thinking about what life would look like if I chose to leave and go my own way. It was hard for me to imagine because the corporate way of life had become so ingrained in me.

Maybe you can identify with some of these feelings. I was afraid that:

- I wouldn't be able to figure out how to start a business.
- I wouldn't like being a business owner or be good at it.
- I wouldn't get any clients.
- I wouldn't make any money.
- I'd be lonely.
- My skills wouldn't transfer into the non-corporate world.
- I wouldn't be able to figure everything out on my own.
- People would say I was crazy for leaving a secure job to go off into the unknown.
- I would regret leaving the safety of my job, and ultimately, fail to be successful.
- Even as an adult woman, I was afraid of what my parents would say!

When You're Not Happy and You Know It

There came a time when my boss was starting to have conversations with me about taking the next step in my career. He was pushing me outside my comfort zone and trying to prepare me to be his successor. He had me work with a business coach to develop my leadership style.

In our coaching sessions, we explored what my natural strengths were and what type of work allowed me to work most "in flow." My coach challenged me to identify the values that I held most strongly, and to craft my own vision statement to guide my life.

The more deeply we explored, the more apparent it became that I was not currently on the right path. This realization left me feeling paralyzed. If I was honest with myself, it meant that I would have to make a big scary decision.

Making the Leap

For many months, I experienced anxiety and uncertainty like I never had before. I felt like an elephant was sitting on my chest, and I couldn't breathe. I constantly had stomachaches. I was faced with the decision of staying with the traditional career path that led me further from my true self or choosing to leave a secure job where I had established credibility and a six-figure salary, all to try something new that I wasn't sure I could pull off.

Ultimately, it was a brief yet very impactful conversation that was the tipping point for me. I'll explain more details of this conversation later, but it was this important conversation that helped me see why I was feeling so badly. I no longer had a choice; I had to follow my calling. The moment had come. I resigned from my job to start my own consulting business.

I have to say that I was extremely fortunate and privileged to have an amazing spouse and a second income that would allow me to have a bit of a buffer to figure it all out. I am very aware that not everyone has this luxury, and this can create additional pressure when starting a new venture. Everyone's situation is unique. You may have a side business that you are considering pursuing full-time, and this would require you to leave your current job and stability. Or you may be in a situation where leaving your job is not your choice at all.

Regardless of your circumstances, I do believe there is significance in "taking a leap of faith" and making the decision as I did. When you make a clear commitment and become emotionally invested in your desires, you put unseen forces into motion. These forces start to align to bring you the information, resources, and people that you need on your journey.

That's exactly what happened to me, and I've seen it happen over and over for others.

You Can Figure It Out

When I finally resigned from my job, I remember feeling like that elephant had finally been lifted off my chest. I could breathe again. It was as if a secret I had been hiding for so long was finally exposed. A flood of emotions came over me in the following weeks. One day I would feel as if I was walking on a cloud with a blank slate of possibility in front of me. I was fired up and ready to build an empire! The next day, I was panicked and questioning if I had made the right choice. I would be instantly filled with self-doubt and question my ability to do anything! And of course, all my well-meaning friends and family were asking me what I was going to do next, and I didn't have an answer more than a weak, "I'm not exactly sure, but I have a bit of an idea…"

You might be experiencing a similar swing of emotions right now (or you're worried you're about to). I want you to know it is completely normal. You have just made a major life decision. It is going to cause some mental turmoil, and you're very likely to notice scattered thoughts and a roller coaster of emotions. You may also feel changes physically as your nervous system is responding to your emotions.

I tried to keep my thoughts focused on the exciting time ahead. I resolved to enjoy some time to recharge myself before starting to work on my business. A couple of weeks later, I received a call out of the blue and was introduced to a potential client by a former colleague. The initial meeting over lunch went well, and I was given my first opportunity to work with a company. I was thrilled—and overwhelmed. Now was the time when I had to create the business that had been forming in my mind.

You may also be feeling this way. The idea of starting a business sounds exciting…but figuring out how to actually do it is another thing!

I remember waking up early one morning and sitting down at the kitchen table staring at a blank piece of paper. I wrote across the top of it "Things I'll need to do to create my business." I started making a list:

- Come up with a business name (no idea)
- Register my business (that sounds like something I probably need to do…)
- Open a bank account (I wonder if I need to do the registration thing first?)
- Create a contract to send to my first client (I guess I need a format to start with)
- Decide what to charge and how to invoice (no clue)

The list flowed out of me, and by the time I was done, I had filled two pages with tasks! I was feeling completely overwhelmed. Regardless of the feeling, I sat back and reminded myself that everything did not have to happen on day one.

I reminded myself that I had been in many situations before where I had thought to myself, "How can I possibly do this?" Much like I had done when my daughter was born prematurely, I reminded myself that I am a person who always figures it out. As the marketing and lifestyle expert Marie Forleo says: "Everything is figureoutable."

This was the first time that I recognized I needed to be the leader of myself. I was the one who had to identify what needed to be done. I was the one who had to direct and coach myself through making it all happen. I was the one who had to find the right resources and people to support me. I was the one who had to keep my thoughts in check and support myself through all the emotions I was feeling. It was all on me. That may sound obvious, but when it really hits you, the weight of that responsibility can feel daunting.

I took my long list and began to prioritize the tasks, breaking them down into smaller, more manageable activities. I focused on only one task at a time. As I started asking questions, the right information, resources, and people showed up to answer them.

I stuck with focusing on one thing at a time. Over the first year, I developed and refined my business and took on my first clients. I successfully delivered several engagements and learned many important lessons. Year after year, I've continued to develop and grow my business and have learned a lot about how to best support myself.

Then and Now: Life on the Other Side

Fast forward to today and this is what my life looks like. I'm sharing this because I want you to see what is possible for you. If you are feeling overwhelmed, it's easy to lose sight of your original reasons or motivation for making the change. Remind yourself to focus on the benefits of the life you are hoping to create.

A Healthier Me

For the fifteen years I spent commuting into the city from the suburbs, I had no idea how much stress it created and the toll it took on my health. I was always tired, unhealthily thin, and caught every illness that was going around. As a mother of two young kids, I was living on caffeine and adrenaline trying to keep everything together. By the time I went through the morning routine of getting everyone ready, dropping kids at two different daycares, and then taking transit to the office, I was often exhausted by the time I sunk into the chair at my desk at 9 am!

Today, my commute is ten steps to my home office—a former backyard shed.

The time I have claimed back creates much more space and calmness in my life. It allows me to spend time doing things that support my health, like walking the neighbourhood trails every morning.

Work Where You Want, When You Want

I am fortunate to now have the freedom to choose when, where, and how I work. I am no longer constrained by traditional office hours or having to physically be somewhere.

I set my own work schedule in a way that works for me. Depending on my schedule, some days I work more hours, and other days I work less. I generally wrap up my workday around 4:30 pm to transition into family life.

Some days I choose to do a yoga class after getting in a few hours of work. I may go for a walk with a friend in the middle of the afternoon or run an errand on the way home from a meeting. On other days I am intensely focused on work and am blind to the rest of the world.

I've been there for my kids when they needed me. I've participated in their school events without feeling guilty or having to ask anyone for permission or time off. I've picked them up when they were sick without having to panic about getting back to the city for work. They have grown up for most of their lives knowing that I am always here for them, and that feels good as a mom.

I can work from anywhere with a WiFi connection. While most of my days are spent working in my home office or at a client's office, some days I work from a coffee shop. As I am writing these words, I am sitting on the deck of our boat looking out at the beautiful fall leaves.

Say Yes to What Lights You Up (and No to the Rest)

In my corporate role, I was given projects to work on, and many times they didn't align with my interests or excite me. Now I get to decide what projects I take on and can focus on work that interests me.

I can also decide which clients I work with—clients who share my values, and those I like and want to support. I don't have to work with any client I don't want to.

Express Your Creative Juices in Rewarding Ways

Something I've learned about myself is that I love to create solutions for problems that I identify. I am no longer constrained to a box of working only on specific types of projects that align with my job description.

If I see a need, I have the freedom to express my creativity by developing an offering to meet that need. As an example, after looking at the stack of unread business books on my bookshelf, a spark of an idea formed, and I followed it.

I launched a membership-based community for business owners called The Business Book Collective. This idea created a new revenue stream and has been very rewarding as I've watched each member learn and excel. I'll share more about how that experience unfolded in a later chapter.

Wave Goodbye to Limits

When it comes to revenue, sometimes there are peaks and valleys, which can feel unsettling. At the same time, I now have unlimited earning potential!

In the corporate world, my earning potential was dictated by a pre-determined scale, and largely depended on the performance of the larger company and my performance against my peers. I can now create my own income, and there are no limits on what is possible.

I've created a financially successful business that has exceeded my corporate income, and I'm focused on continuing to grow and expand.

Time for Personal Growth

Over the years I've invested in several conferences and training programs that have expanded my skills and ways of thinking. I get to decide what is right for me. I can pursue the things that interest me most without having to get approval from a professional development department.

In the last couple of years, I've invested heavily in studying mindset, primarily through a program called Thinking Into Results created by Bob Proctor. My personal growth as a result of this study has been life-changing. It has helped me to grow my business and take on meaningful projects like writing this book, a bucket list goal that I previously wouldn't have had the courage or confidence to pursue.

A Whole New World of Relationships

I've dramatically expanded my sphere of relationships through the clients I've worked with, the various entrepreneurial groups

I'm involved in, and the relationships I've established with vendors and owners of complementary businesses. My network is rich and diverse, and I've formed many deep friendships with like-minded entrepreneurs.

The Raw Truth

Now for a dose of reality. It has not always been rainbows and sunshine. Along with all the positive shifts, there have been many challenging days of struggle. I've taken on projects I shouldn't have, and I've paid the price by managing difficult clients. I've underestimated the time commitment on projects and ended up working for next to free. I've panicked when I didn't have the next project lined up as I watched my revenue dip.

I've said yes too much and ended up at my desk until midnight for weeks on end, burning myself out. I've had many sleepless nights berating myself for things I did or didn't do, and I have gone through phases where I doubted my abilities. I've invested in technology that turned out to be a waste of money and launched offerings that flopped.

I've had many days when I've thought to myself, "Maybe I should just get a regular job. It would be so much easier!"

When you have days like this, I want you to remember what I'm about to share.

It's All Worth It

There is an important distinction between my former life and my current life. I am now in the driver's seat choosing the direction for my life, like you are now or soon will be. We get to spend our precious amount of time on this earth doing work that is meaningful and makes a real impact. That knowledge creates an unbelievable level of personal fulfillment and makes the hard work worth it.

What ties most people to traditional employment is the feeling of security it provides. But the reality is that job security is a thing of the past. I find more security in knowing that I can create my future without having to rely on a single employer. Knowing what I know now, choosing to start my own business was one of the best decisions I ever made. If I hadn't moved past my fears, I would have never known the life I have now, and that would have been a shame.

I also feel very grateful knowing that I have been able to be an example for my children of what carving your own path looks like. I feel this is especially important for my daughter because I want her to understand that life doesn't have to look one way if you want it to look another.

That's enough about me. Let's start on *you!*

PART 1

Start by Getting Clear

IN THIS SECTION, WE WILL EXPLORE SEVERAL topics that will help you bring clarity and order to your mind. We will talk about stepping into your new role as a business owner and evolving your self-image.

We will also talk about ways to uncover what lights you up—as this knowledge is a key to thriving. We will then spend time getting clear on your values, which will form the foundation of your business. From there, we'll develop a vision for your business.

We will end with a personal story of how the relationship I have with myself has changed through my mindset journey. I will encourage you to explore areas in your life that might be creating mental clutter.

Going through the topics in this section will help set you up to unpack concepts related to mindset and give you clarity about where you're heading.

Chapter 1

Stepping into the New You

ONE OF THE MOST CRITICAL SHIFTS THAT NEEDS to be made when moving from employee to business owner is how you see yourself. Entrepreneurship requires you to take on a whole new identity, oftentimes an identity that is very different. This transition can shock the core of your being, as how you see yourself can have a direct impact on your results in ways you might not be aware of.

When you were an employee, you had a certain internal experience regarding your thoughts and beliefs. As a leader of your own business, you will have a very different internal experience.

For example, as an employee, you are rewarded by validation from others. Employees are extrinsically motivated to complete a task by the positive feedback they will receive from management. As a business owner, you will need to draw motivation from an intrinsic place. There is nobody to pat you on the back and praise your good work. You will need to become your own cheerleader, celebrating yourself for taking initiative and accomplishing goals in a way that may not come naturally (given your past conditioning).

ENTREPRENEUR INSIGHT

From Earner to Creator

In the corporate world, you earn based on the results you create. You are validated and rewarded for reaching the goals your employer sets, and it becomes ingrained in you to please the hand that feeds you.

As an entrepreneur, you must shift into a different dynamic where your rewards are more internally driven by what you yourself create. When I left my corporate role, I didn't realize how much of my identity was programmed to be an employee defined by a title and paycheque. Making the mental shift from an earner to a creator was a huge adjustment and a conscious undertaking for me.

— Laura D'Andrea, *Co-Owner, Smudge Allot Inc.*

Many women coming out of traditional employment jump straight into doing all of the things their logical mind tells them is necessary to do when building a business. Often unknowingly, they try to bypass doing the internal work first. If the way you think isn't aligned with your actions, the disconnect can result in both a waste of time and money.

A more connected approach is to understand the way you will need to think about yourself in your new role, followed by working on the internalization of this new you. By doing the mindset work first, you will bring better energy to the experience of creating your business. You will feel more settled and more confident in your new role, and as a result, you will also become more effective.

Prepare to Expand

In your traditional employment setting or corporate environment, you lived in a world that likely had a hierarchal structure, and you were paid an hourly wage or a salary. Your primary focus was on delivering your expertise within a larger organization. Your focus was on being a "doer of things," or the technician of your own expertise. Your boss set your priorities, and you likely worked with and contributed to a team.

You had narrow responsibility for doing the things you were good at, and you probably had access to people and resources with complementary skill sets who could support you in accomplishing your goals. There were other people in the company with roles that focused on each area of running the business, like operations, finance, and marketing.

As a business owner, you are not only responsible for delivering your expertise, but you are also responsible for taking on additional roles to lead and manage the business.

One of the books I read early in my entrepreneurial journey was *The E-Myth Revisited* by Michael Gerber. The book's central message is that most businesses fail because of the "entrepreneurial myth." The author tells of the misconception that having great technical skills also makes one good at running a business. This is not true.

The author explains that business owners need to take on three key roles in their business:

- The *Technician* role: focusing on doing the work, and selling and delivering it
- The *Manager* role: focusing on people and systems
- The *Entrepreneurial Visionary* role: focusing on planning the future of the business

Become a Master Builder

Understanding that you are now responsible for embodying, adapting to, and balancing all three roles will be critical to your success. However, to be clear, this does not mean you will always be required to do the work of all three roles, or that you need to be an expert in every aspect related to your business.

You need to take on the mindset of being the "Master Builder" of your business—a term I learned while working with my construction clients.

In early Roman times, building projects were overseen by someone with the title of Master Builder. This person was the central figure and held the vision for the overall project. They had a level of proficiency in various building trades, created project plans, and oversaw the execution of the work. You are the Master Builder for your business!

Balance Your Key Roles

It is common for people to get caught up in the "doer" role because it feels most familiar and comfortable given one's previous experience. However, in doing so, they often neglect the visionary and manager roles. This may especially be true if you hold the belief that you are "not a businessperson" or you are "not good at business." This belief can be amplified if you are coming into entrepreneurship from a creative role, or if you consider creativity and business skills to be opposites.

Another key concept shared in *The E-Myth Revisited* is that business owners need to spend time working "on the business," as opposed to working "in the business." When you are working "in the business," you are serving in your role as the Technician and delivering your product or service. When you are working "on the business" you are spending time in your role as the Manager and Entrepreneurial Visionary.

When playing the three key roles, it is critical to find balance in the time you spend working *in* and *on* the business. While you will naturally be drawn to one of the three key roles, you must learn to maneuver between each or find people to work with you in a complementary way. This could mean hiring someone or finding a coach or mentor to guide you.

Your Inner Thoughts Create Your Outer Self

With a better understanding of the roles you will need to take on, let's focus on matching your inner thinking to support those roles.

Bob Proctor, who was considered the world's foremost expert on the human mind, taught extensively about the concept of "self-image" because he believed it to be the foundation for our thinking. He explained that we first have our outer image, which is the way the world sees us and the way others experience us; and second is our inner self-image, which is our own perception of ourselves. Our inner self-image includes the thoughts we repeatedly think, as well as the beliefs we hold about ourselves.

Your self-image has been programmed into your subconscious mind through both your DNA and through the experiences you have lived. In a later chapter, we will talk more about how your subconscious mind operates. For now, I want you to understand that this inner self-image acts as a control mechanism that determines both your actions and your results. Bob always shared that we can never grow beyond our self-image.

For example, if you think of yourself as a shy person, you will be quieter in conversations or hesitant to introduce yourself to new people. If you shift your self-image to being someone that is more outgoing, you will, over time, become more naturally open and comfortable meeting new people. You will hold yourself more confidently, and you will be more engaging in social situations.

A fascinating example that demonstrates the power of self-image is shared in *Psycho-Cybernetics* by Maxwell Maltz, a plastic surgeon in the 1960s who first began to work with the idea of self-image. He observed that when he operated on patients to correct some form of imperfection, in some cases the person's self-perception would change. In other cases, it would not. Through his research, he came to understand that we have two images: the one we see in the mirror, and the one we hold in our minds.

To understand the image you hold in your mind now, start taking notice of the thoughts that come up in your internal chatter, and how you refer to yourself in conversations with others. When you hear yourself starting sentences with, "I'm not the kind of person who…" or "I just always…" take a mental note. For example, things like, "I'm not the kind of person who is good at reaching out to new people," or "I'm not a good public speaker," are clues to the internal self-image you are holding.

The good news is that your self-image can be reprogrammed to support the required growth in your new role as a business owner. You can quite literally write the script of who you need to become to achieve the vision you have for your business. You then program that version of yourself into your subconscious mind through repetition until you truly believe it. With each repetition, you are laying down new neural patterns in your brain, and as a result, your mind is becoming reprogrammed. Being a successful business owner can become a part of your core identity.

Write, Read, Repeat

Creating a self-image or self-identity script can be a powerful exercise to transform the way you think about yourself. Start by setting aside time to consider the qualities you would like to embody. Think about the qualities you will need in order to bring the vision you have for your business to life. Look at people who are successful, or those who you admire, and identify some of their traits and the ways they show up in the world. It could be someone you know or a public figure.

BUSINESS INSIGHT

There Are No Rules

Women can struggle with defining themselves as being "successful in business" because society has defined "success" in a way that stems from a patriarchal system. Women can feel as though they need to adopt a stereotypically "male" attitude toward business: being hyper-driven, competitive, or aggressive.

Without successful female role models in your life, it can be difficult to envision being successful while still remaining true to yourself. The beautiful truth is this: there are no rules. You get to define who you are as a business owner. You can be focused and kind. You can be driven and collaborative. You can be your own version of a business owner—and a successful one at that!

The traits you admire in others…you may be unaware of it, but they are also buried somewhere inside you. They might be buried under false beliefs, and you might not be able to recognize them yet. But they are there, waiting for you to uncover them.

When you think of people you consider role models (models of the kind of business owner you would like to be), begin to answer some questions about the attributes you are drawn to:

- How would you describe their personality?

- What do you think they believe about themselves and their business?

- How do they carry themselves when they show up in a room?
- What consistent actions do they take in their business?
- What attitude do they bring to situations?

Start cherry-picking the attributes you think can support you in your growth.

Next, think about what your ideal life looks like. Give yourself permission to dream and think about all the things you want to bring into your life. These may include:

- I have a close relationship with my children. I am here for them whenever they need me, without asking anyone for permission.
- I have an amazing relationship with my partner because we have a lunch date every Friday.
- Top-tier brands are on a waiting list to work with me!
- I live in the bright and modern home I always wanted.

Capture the list.

Now, look at both lists and let your pen flow. Write about the version of you that you will become—or more accurately, that you will uncover.

You may find it easier to begin by writing in the third person, almost as if you are creating a fictional character. Later, change the "she" to "I" to make it personal, and create a series of short statements you feel connected to. These statements should excite and motivate you, and make you feel powerful. For example:

- I am a natural leader that inspires and guides others.
- I effortlessly attract clients that happily pay me a premium.
- I exude a confidence and joy that is infectious.

The whole purpose of the script is to stir up an emotional connection. Use words or phrases that evoke feelings for you. Become emotionally involved in the exercise and really try to feel it. The more chills you get, the better!

Every day, read and write out your script. Doing so repetitively will give your subconscious mind the direction it needs to begin experiencing this new version of yourself.

Record yourself reading it aloud and play it back repeatedly. Practice saying it to yourself in the mirror, and really focus on embodying the feelings the script brings up. The more repetition, the better, as your subconscious mind is programmed through repetition.

Get ready to welcome *her*—the new you—into your life as she begins to emerge.

REFLECTIONS

What are your key takeaways from this chapter?

What new ideas will you commit to trying or implementing in your business?

Chapter 2

Know What Lights You Up

IT IS IMPORTANT TO REFLECT SPECIFICALLY ON the ways in which you work best. Only when you are clear in your own mind about who you are can you effectively communicate what makes you different. With this clarity, you can also structure your business in a way that allows you to do work that lights you up.

When working in alignment with your innate gifts, you can be of the highest service by showing up as a complete *you*. You will feel more fulfilled and settled internally because you are leveraging what comes most naturally to you. This is an essential contributor to cultivating what makes you thrive.

You have strengths and qualities you were born with, and you have abilities that you developed through your experience as an employee. Your abilities and expertise give you superpowers that you will bring to your business.

Discover Yourself and Leverage Your Language

Spend some time reflecting on each job you've had throughout your life. Look beyond the titles and write a list of all the things you accomplished in the roles. In what areas did you excel, and what areas excited you the most? Create a similar list of accomplishments such as life experiences and volunteer work, or the ways in which you have helped others. On both lists, think about the roles or projects you loved and compare them to the ones you struggled to get through.

Now review everything you have written and seek out the common themes or characteristics you displayed. These will be of value to highlight in your business.

In doing this exercise for myself, I saw that I take joy from asking questions to find clarity and connecting dots that others might not see. I'm good at distilling things down to their simplest form. I enjoy project-based work and building relationships. I don't love managing large teams or repetitive tasks. I also noted that I am energized when working on multiple projects, and I am most fired up when creating something new.

There are many personality-profiling books that come with assessments. These can be helpful in fleshing out what makes you unique, and they can provide you with language to help express that. Having a clear understanding of yourself can help you create a business that aligns with you. It will also be something you draw on to create engaging marketing messaging.

The first book I recommend is called *StrengthsFinder 2.0: Discover Your CliftonStrengths* from Gallup and Tom Rath (now *CliftonStrengths by Gallup*) which comes with access to an online assessment. It is a short but highly informative book. The assessment helps you to uncover your talents so you can focus on further developing them.

This assessment helped me create the first tagline I used when launching my own business: "Focused Strategy. Disciplined Execution." This tagline encompassed both my strengths and what my clients were looking for. In interviews with my ideal clients, I heard people talking about how they felt their marketing was lacking focus and strategy. They also expressed frustration in their inability to execute their ideas due to a lack of skills or capacity.

Sally Hogshead takes a different spin from the above in her book *Fascinate: How to Make Your Brand Impossible to Resist,* which also includes an online assessment. Her approach is based not only on strengths, but also on how what you offer is unique because of how you, the person, are essential to the solution you are providing. This understanding can help you to see how the world sees you in a specific way.

Another helpful free online assessment is called the Sparketype™ assessment. This, along with the companion book, *Sparked: Discover Your Unique Imprint for Work that Makes You Come Alive* by Jonathan Fields, can help you identify the work that makes you feel "fully expressed, alive with purpose, and absorbed in flow."

We Are All Designed Uniquely

And finally, another tool that has helped me understand how I draw energy from my work is using something called Human Design. This tool offers a map of your unique genetic design. It is based on astrology and aligns your profile with your exact time and date of birth. This might be too far out for you, but I'm sharing it because it has been very validating for me, helping me to understand myself in a new light.

I learned I am a profile called a Manifesting Generator. This essentially means that I am a multi-passionate creator gifted with bringing ideas to life quickly. I am capable of having my energy in many things at once. That pretty much sums up who I am! If you ask me what I am up to on any given day, it is usually a varied list.

This explains why entrepreneurship is a good fit for me. It allows me to create solutions and work with multiple clients and on multiple projects simultaneously. This knowledge of how I function best has also helped me understand why I get energized in the creation process but lose interest in things over time.

I used to see this as a fault, but now I see it as one of my gifts, and this new perspective is very freeing. I've now designed my business to reflect how I work best, in a way that delivers what is of most value to my clients. By understanding that my best skills are clarifying and creating, I have structured my primary service offerings around providing strategies, assessments, and road maps. I then work with other people to oversee the execution of key projects, and eventually move them into an in-house role while I move into an advisory role.

Pull it All Together

Through drawing on information from the various assessments and knowledge gained from self-reflection, you will begin to develop a deeper understanding of who you are and be clearer in your mind. This knowledge will feel empowering, and it will allow you to make better decisions from day one about how to structure your business and support yourself during projects.

Writing this book, for example, drew on much of what lights me up. It was a project that had a beginning and an end. I drew on my capabilities to distill a great deal of information down to what I think are the most important topics to cover. I drew on my Manifesting Generator energy to create the first draft in a very condensed timeframe because I was motivated to get this information out into the world.

When you go through the exercise of learning more about your personality and motivators, you may find that what lights you up is very different from what lights me up. You may be most energized by abstract thinking and collaborating with others. If you took on the project of writing a book, you might engage a ghostwriter to turn your thoughts into words. Or you might choose to collaborate with other experts to create a book in which each chapter is contributed by individual authors. The result is still creating a book, but by a different path to get there. Identify the option that allows you to draw on your natural abilities and enjoy the process.

I hope you can see how developing a better understanding of who you are is an important step in creating a business that reflects what works for you. I'd encourage you to take some of the assessments I've shared or find others that will be helpful for you. Once you have done so, you might go back to your self-image script and make some tweaks.

REFLECTIONS

What are your key takeaways from this chapter?

What new ideas will you commit to trying or implementing in your business?

Chapter 3

Paint the Picture of Your Vision

NOW THAT YOU UNDERSTAND WHAT MAKES YOU unique and how you work best, let's begin connecting those understandings to the business you are creating. In this chapter, I'll lead you through some questions to intentionally create the kind of business and life you want. After all, you don't just want to create a business; you want to create a business that allows you to thrive and be successful on your own terms.

We're also going to tap into one of your most powerful mindset tools, your imagination, to paint a picture of the vision you have for your business and life.

What Does 'Thriving' Mean to You?

In the sub-title of this book, I used the phrase "become a thriving entrepreneur." I invite you to take some time to reflect on what "thriving" means to you.

When you end the day feeling satisfied and fulfilled, like your cup is full and your energy has been spent in a good way, think back and ask yourself what happened to put you in that place? How did you spend your day? What words would you use to describe that feeling of thriving?

Everyone has their own definition of thriving. Decide on yours so you can recognize the feeling that you are working toward creating in your life.

Creating the Right Business for You and Your Clients

When it comes to the nature of your business, you have 100 percent creative freedom. A business can look many ways, and your vision will continue to evolve over time as you continue to grow as a person.

As you go through the following questions, think about what your business would need to look like to express who you are and allow you to thrive.

- What do you want out of the experience of starting your own business?
- Do you want to have a certain income or reach a certain level of financial abundance?
- Do you want to make an impact in a specific way?
- What is the thing you love to do that helps others?
- How can you help someone experience an outcome or transformation through your business?
- What do you want your clients to get out of the experience of working with you?
- Through which method do you want to serve your clients? Do you want to work face-to-face with people, or in an online setting?
- Do you want to serve a small group of people individually, or do you want to create a business that is scalable to reach larger audiences?
- What do you want your typical day to look like?

- Do you want to work alone, or do you want to build a team?

- Do you want to provide customized solutions, or repeatable ones?

Answering these questions will help you start to build a vision for both your business and your life. Having a clear picture in your mind of what you are working toward will propel you forward in an intentional way.

This vision will help you to make decisions today that will serve you in the future. For example, if you plan to offer a service that can be delivered individually, what would it look like if you were going to deliver that service to fifty people simultaneously? Are there things you can be doing from day one to set yourself up for the expanded version of that offering?

BUSINESS INSIGHT

Align Your Business Model with Your Vision

Your business model will define how you deliver a product or service in exchange for payment that creates revenue, and ultimately, profit. You may have multiple models within your business that provide different income streams.

Give some thought to the model that best aligns with who you are and what your vision is. Examples of business models include:

- Retail or E-commerce: You sell individual products in a brick and mortar store or through an online shop.

- Subscription-based: You sell a product or service on a recurring basis for a monthly fee.

- Consulting-based: You are hired for your expertise to provide advice and guidance. You are compensated on an hourly, retainer, or project basis.

- Agency-based: You bring people together—either employees or freelancers—to deliver expertise or done-for-you services to complete a specific task. In this model, you may deliver some of the services yourself, or you may focus only on your role of leading the agency.

- Online education: Clients can access live or pre-recorded educational content through an online platform.

- Group coaching program: Clients can access educational or developmental resources, a community of like-minded individuals, and support alongside other clients.

Keep in mind the business you are creating on day one and remember to factor in potential for growth in the future through a scalable model. For example, you may start with a coaching-based model and later develop an online course that can be delivered on-demand or as a group coaching program.

Visualization Is the First Step toward Actualization

The imagination can be a powerful tool. Creating images in our minds and infusing them with emotion is the first step to bringing them about in the world.

In *Your Invisible Power,* Genevieve Behrend shared, "Everyone visualizes, whether they know it or not. Visualizing is the great secret of Success. The conscious use of this great power attracts to you greatly multiplied resources, intensifies your wisdom, and enables you to make use of advantages which you formerly failed to recognize."

Using your imagination to tap into the feeling of achieving your vision or goal is a powerful mindset tool.

As a companion resource for this chapter, I invite you to enjoy the guided visualization created by my mindset coach. This will help you engage your imagination toward creating a rich vision for your life and business.

ENTREPRENEUR INSIGHT

Believe It to See It

If you have not had the experience of guided visualization, you are in for a treat!

Carve out some time and a quiet space to enjoy the visualization exercise that can be downloaded here: www.goodtogrowmarketing. ca/bookresources.

— Catherine Farquharson, *Mindset & Transformation Coach*

After completing the visualization, do you have a clear vision? Are you connected to how you want to feel once you have achieved the vision?

To Reach Success You Must Define Success

With your vision in mind, I suggest you spend some time refining, and likely expanding, your definition of "success" to reflect your new world.

In your previous life, your success was largely measured by your income, your title, and your ability to move through the ranks of a hierarchal structure. With those measures now gone, you need to create a new definition of success that fits with your vision.

Your success may now be more defined by the impact you make or the life experience you create. While some people want to build a business that can scale to reach significant revenue, others want to create a business that provides a certain level of income accompanied by freedom to focus on other areas of life, such as family.

Yes, success may mean reaching a certain financial goal, but that isn't the only thing to consider. You may want to create a business where you invest only twenty hours each week, allowing you to allocate time to your family or other interests.

Success might mean having the ability to work from anywhere so you can incorporate more travel into your lifestyle. It might mean knowing you can structure your time in a way that allows you to pick your kids up from school every day or care for an aging parent. Or maybe success means having the freedom to choose your work and the ability to express your creativity.

Everyone has their own definition of success. Think about what success looks like for you in both big and little ways. You don't have to aim to build an empire. Or, if building an empire is what you want, go for it! It's up to you. Just remember not to get caught up in the Instagram story of someone else's definition of success. Create your own—one that works for you.

Your One-Sentence Vision

Sum up your vision into a simple statement that focuses on the outcome of what you are creating and elicits emotion in you. This statement will become a touchstone that you go back to for guidance. It will be what gets you up in the morning, and what keeps you moving forward when there are bumps in the road.

This is your *why*. When you have to push through a fear or do something that feels uncomfortable, this is what you will come back to as a reminder of *why* you are doing what you are doing.

Here are a few examples:

My vision for this book is to "Inspire and empower women to become thriving entrepreneurs and create a life they love."

If you are an HR consultant, your vision might be to "Support the underdogs by giving small businesses the same access to HR strategies that large companies enjoy."

A content strategist I work with has a beautiful vision to "Share good stories that help responsible brands make a greater impact."

REFLECTIONS

What are your key takeaways from this chapter?

What new ideas will you commit to trying or implementing in your business?

Chapter 4

Get Solid on Your Values

YOUR VALUES REPRESENT THE BELIEFS YOU HOLD close to your heart and what you stand for in the world. They guide your behaviour and act as your code of conduct. They are an intrinsic aspect of who you are, rather than something you decide to be. As your business is an extension of you, it will naturally be a reflection of your values.

Uncovering and articulating your values can help you understand what matters the most to you, and how you want to show up in your business. When you stay true to your values, you feel aligned; when you don't, you feel incongruent. Being misaligned can lead to poor decision-making or having an unsettled feeling during interactions.

Have you ever been in a situation where you felt like something was off, but you couldn't exactly identify what it was? That is often a sign that you are out of alignment with your values. It was a misalignment of values that ultimately led me to leave my corporate job.

When Your Values Don't Match

Before leaving my corporate role, I went through an exercise with a business coach to identify my values. She handed me a deck of about fifty cards, and on each card, the names of different values were written. She asked me to flip through the deck and pull the cards that I felt like I resonated with. Through a process of elimination, she had me narrow my choice down to six cards. It was not easy!

I identified six values for myself: independence, authenticity, kindness, integrity, family, and health. After identifying these values, I began to understand why I was feeling out of alignment in my career. This became very apparent in the conversation that I mentioned before—the conversation that was ultimately the tipping point that led to my resignation.

I was in a meeting with a group of people discussing plans for a project. When the most senior person in the room put forward her point of view, I could feel my blood begin to boil. The proposal she was suggesting would make her look good, but it would not have resulted in a valuable outcome. Tactfully, I asked, "Maybe it would be more effective to direct the budget towards research with our clients?" She responded, "Yes, it would be great if we could also do client research, but this budget has already been earmarked for internal research to get feedback on how our department is viewed by the partners."

When I left the meeting, my boss could see I was upset after having my question dismissed, and he invited me to sit with him for a coffee. I told him how frustrated I was that we couldn't use the funds allocated for research to get more data on our clients in order to develop more effective marketing. I can remember so clearly the words he spoke. He said, "You know what your problem is? You care too much." I felt like time stood still as I absorbed his words. He said, "You need to let things roll off your back and play the game. Go home to your family at night and don't worry about it."

But it wasn't that easy for me. Caring about my work and feeling like I was making a difference were important to me.

Working for a company that appreciated how much I cared also mattered to me. I realized in that moment that I was not being valued for sharing my authentic self, and that I was compromising my integrity by staying in a job that required me to be someone I wasn't.

The next day I called in sick, and sat at my kitchen table in tears trying to decide what to do. Deep down I knew that what I was experiencing was a misalignment of values, and I was terrified about what it meant. I had some deep conversations with my husband, and I had a call with my business coach.

My coach could sense I was at an important crossroads in my life but knew that fear was holding me back from choosing which path I would take. She asked me to think of someone who I considered fearless. I identified my daughter Stella. She was eight years old at the time and already had a free-spirited attitude that, to be honest, often made me crazy as a parent. However, I knew that this characteristic would serve her well in life. She was willing to try anything, and if she failed, she would just shrug her shoulders and move on.

My coach asked me to put myself in Stella's shoes and think about the decision she would make. As I thought about the answer, I looked up and saw a piece of artwork that Stella had made hanging on the wall. It was a rainbow of colours with a line written on each colour. She had written: "I am little. I like green. I can do anything."

As I read the last line, I knew which decision I had to make. At that moment, I decided. It was time to build a business that aligned with my values.

Uncover Your Values

I encourage you to spend some time thinking about your own values. The article in this section provides an approach that is slightly different from the exercise I went through, but it does provide another way to achieve the same outcome.

ENTREPRENEUR INSIGHT

A Simple Exercise to Mine Your Values

I worked for a company where I had a values mismatch, so defining my own values was an important first step in creating my business. Here's a simple practice to uncover your own values that was shared by my coach at the Art of Excellence.

Separate a fresh piece of paper into three columns. In the first column write the names of three to five people you admire. This can be anyone, someone in your life now, or someone who has passed, someone you know intimately or someone who you wish you could meet. I've seen all answers from my mom or my manager to Mother Teresa, Elvis, and Martin Luther King. The important thing is that they are someone you admire.

In the second column write next to each person what you admire about them. Is it how they handle themselves in the world? Maybe they take great care of the people around them. Maybe they are driven to their goals? What do you admire most about them?

In the last column write down all the values you feel they possess. If you are struggling with this one because you can't come up with the name of the value, Google "list of values" and several lists to choose from will come up.

Review the list to look for patterns in the values. Choose a short-list of words that have repeated, or you feel strongly about, and start narrowing them down for yourself until you get to three to five values.

When I did this exercise, I had one of the values only show up once, but I felt so strongly about it that I added it to my list of five. Mine are Strength, Drive, Integrity, Care for others, and Vision.

The last step in the process is to define the words for yourself. When I say drive, it means constantly moving forward and being better. Over the years the definition has changed a bit. While it's still a value for me, it doesn't look like pushing my body to the limit in sports. Now it looks more like learning and meeting goals I set for myself. Be clear yourself about what each value means to you.

> — Lisa Wilson, *Human Resource Cultural Consultant and Leadership Coach, LMW Consultation*

In your business, your values will serve as a filter in many important ways. These may include:

- Deciding if you are aligned on values with a potential client.
- Screening potential employees or freelancers to work with.
- Helping to prioritize both your projects and your time.
- Functioning as a litmus test when evaluating partners to work with.

I had an experience a few years into my business that taught me an important lesson in working with strategic partners who align with my values.

A consultant invited me to join him to meet with a potential client because he felt the client had needs in his area of expertise, but also that they could use my help with their marketing. As we lived close to one another, he suggested we drive into the city together.

At the start of the meeting, the consultant I arrived with was very gracious in his introduction, and helped the potential client feel comfortable with me. About halfway through the meeting, it became obvious that the client had chosen not to work with the consultant I arrived with, but that they did wish to work with me to meet their marketing needs. The consultant's demeanour immediately shifted when he discovered this. I could see him becoming irritated and wanting to wrap up.

When we left the meeting, he said he had another meeting downtown and asked me, "You're okay to make your own way back home, right?" I was completely caught off guard and simply nodded my head yes, not knowing what else to say.

It was very clear that because he was not going to get an engagement out of the meeting, he was done with the pursuit… and with me. He left me standing in the snow in the middle of February. As I thought I would only be in and out of a car, I had worn only a light coat and heels not made for walking to the subway.

This interaction spoke volumes to me about this person's values—values that obviously did not align with my own values of integrity and kindness. I made my way home in the snow that day and decided I would not accept any future referrals from this consultant. We were clearly not aligned.

Get clear on your values and use them as your guide.

REFLECTIONS

What are your key takeaways from this chapter?

What new ideas will you commit to trying or implementing in your business?

Chapter 5

Clear Your Mental Clutter

THERE IS A SUBTLE BUT IMPORTANT CONNECTION between the way you feel about yourself and the success you will experience in your business. If you do not have a good internal relationship with yourself, it will create mental clutter. Or, if there are things in your life that you are not dealing with, they will take up valuable mind space.

At the end of the day, *you* are the one creating this business. You must support yourself every step of the way. The first step is to nurture the most important relationship you have: the one with yourself.

ENTREPRENEUR INSIGHT

Business growth comes with personal growth. When I started my business, I thought personal growth was super 'woo-woo' and I just needed to focus on hard business. I now know better and regularly read personal development books, set goals for myself, and vocalize spots where I feel I need personal growth.

— Cari Brunton, *Owner, Red Bucket Events*

In this chapter, I'll share a very personal story about how I came to understand the importance of dealing with the things in your life that take up mental space, and the necessity of healing your relationship with yourself. Your story may be different from mine. For you, it might be a bad relationship with another person, or something else that makes you feel like you have something you need to resolve.

Whatever it is, start working through it so it doesn't take up headspace, because otherwise, it will affect your ability to confidently build your business. You may be able to move through it on your own or you may need help. As you are reading my story, think about what areas in your life may have mental clutter that needs to be cleared.

A Lifelong Obsession

Since early in my childhood, around age seven, I've had a poor relationship with my body. I think it began as I became aware of my body, and as adults started to make comments about it. I learned to equate being thin with being good. Being thin was something you were praised and loved for. This was a bit of a contradiction in my family culture, where food (often unhealthy but very yummy German food) was central to all our family gatherings and celebrations.

I remember feeling like I didn't look like the other girls and wanting desperately to fit in. Looking back at old photographs breaks my heart because I can now see that I was a beautiful child. But as I look at those photographs, I can also clearly remember the thoughts in my head as a child.

I went on my first diet in fourth grade. That diet kicked off a lifelong quest to "fix" myself, and I was constantly on one program or another. One day I was vegetarian, the next Keto, and soon onto trying the South Beach Diet. All the while, I was torturing myself and beating myself up in my head for never getting it right.

The way we talk to ourselves internally has a dramatic impact on our sense of self-worth and confidence. This impact isn't just isolated to our bodies. It trickles into all areas of our lives, including our careers and businesses.

A Shift in Thinking

As an adult, most of my brain activity focused on berating myself about my body. I obsessed over what I disliked, or what I wanted to fix. And I obsessed about food: what I could or couldn't eat, and what I was going to eat next. These obsessions consumed my mind for most of my life without me even realizing there was another way.

Then one day when I went for breakfast with my sister, I was looking at the menu trying to decide what to order. I started eliminating one item after the other in my mind. My sister turned to me and asked, "Oh, so what can you eat here? You're Keto, right? Or is it low-carb?" I had a dizzying moment where I couldn't remember what label I was ascribing to at the time. Then I heard a faint voice in my head say, "Or you could just eat food." I thought to myself, *What? What kind of crazy concept is that?!*

Shortly after, I came across a book called *Healthy as F*ck* by Oonagh Duncan, in which I found a line that changed everything for me. The author said, "No one ever hated themselves into a body they loved." She said women make a mistake because they have their relationship with their body backwards. They decide they will be happy only when they reach a certain goal, like a number on the scale.

Instead, we must strive to be happy where we are now. We must simply love our bodies as they are, because that is the feeling we are after anyways. It is not about the number on the scale. It is about how you think you will feel when you reach that number.

This realization hit me like a ton of bricks. I had spent my life hating my body, and by extension, hating myself because I couldn't fix it. I was basing my happiness on my body looking a certain way or seeing a certain number on the scale. By allowing how I felt about my body to hold me back, I was robbing myself of so many experiences in my life. I wasn't present in experiences or appreciative of my successes because my brain was on negative chatter autopilot.

I decided to do an experiment. I would ditch my scale, drop my numerous food rules, and simply try just eating intuitively for a while. I wanted to try being kinder to myself to see what happened. I followed my inner guidance about what I felt like eating and how it made me feel. I started looking at exercise as being less about torturing myself and more about moving because it felt good. I unsubscribed to all the diet and weight loss feeds I was following on social media.

I became very aware of my self-talk (and mortified by it!) and shut down the negative voice whenever I caught it. I found things to appreciate about my body and approached the relationship with more love and compassion. I told myself over and over that I love my body exactly how it is today. I focused on doing things that made me feel good, like walking in the forest every day.

A New Experience

Here is the interesting thing that happened as a result of clearing my mental clutter, and how it relates to my business. As I worked on being kinder to myself, it was as if I began peeling back the layers of an onion. The negative chatter in my brain was quieter. The mind can focus on only one thing at a time. Without the incessant obsession with my body and food, I slowly started to free up space to think about other things—things like my business!

I made room for hearing inspiring thoughts and was able to think more creatively and come up with new ideas to expand my business into other areas. I felt lighter in my relationship with my body, and ultimately, I felt much happier. My sense of self-worth and confidence grew stronger. I have much more compassion and love for myself today. It is still a work in progress, but living in my head is a much more pleasant experience these days.

What's taking up your mind space? What are you brushing under the rug or not dealing with that could be costing you your confidence and ability to grow into your full potential? What do you need to address in your life to free yourself to grow into the happiest and most effective version of you?

It's not always a big issue or trauma that occupies your mind. Sometimes it's a combination of little things that you keep putting off dealing with. You get frustrated with yourself whenever you step into your messy closet or sit down in your disorganized office. The little things you put off dealing with create tiny energy leaks that drain your energy over time.

Make a list of the things taking up your mental energy and start taking small steps to address them.

REFLECTIONS

What are your key takeaways from this chapter?

What new ideas will you commit to trying or implementing in your business?

PART 2

Make Your Mind Work for You

YOU HAVE A CHOICE TO MAKE: you can live in a constant battle with your mind while building your business, or you can choose to learn to work with your mindset.

Having picked up this book, I assume you are on board for the second option!

In this section, I'll explain how your mind works, and provide you with some ideas and tools to consider adopting. We will talk about the parts of your mind and how you can work with your subconscious mind to change habits. We will talk about energy, and I will introduce you to some (possibly) new ideas about working with energy and the universe. We will then dive into understanding the power of your beliefs. I will also share some tools to help you form habits that will support your mindset day-to-day.

I could write a book on each chapter! If you have studied personal development, you may be familiar with some of the following ideas. If not, I encourage you to stay open-minded. I've tried to share some big concepts in bite-sized chunks with accompanying examples. I hope this section will pique your interest and provide you with ideas to further explore in your mindset journey.

Chapter 6

Embrace Your Magical Mind

IN THIS CHAPTER, I'M GOING TO SHARE SOME concepts that helped me understand how our minds work, and how the mind impacts our ability to change our habits and lives. At the mention of the word "mind," most people think of the brain. The brain, however, is just an organ in the body.

We commonly use the word "brain" interchangeably with "mind," but these two are not the same. Without an understanding of how the mind works, you will likely experience success on a hit-and-miss basis. However, with an understanding of how the mind works, you can use it to your advantage to create success consistently.

Unlike the brain, the mind permeates every cell of your body, and expresses itself through the body. We will focus on two parts of the mind that control what we think, say, feel and do: the conscious mind and the subconscious mind.

The conscious mind is the *thinking* mind. It uses the five senses to interact with the physical world and is responsible for our mental processing. When we try to use our thinking mind to change our behaviour, we often find ourselves back where we started, wondering why we failed again.

The subconscious mind is the *feeling* mind. It is responsible for most of our actions, and we are not even aware of it. It is programmed through our experiences, often starting at a very young age. Behaviours you learned from watching your parents and those around you do things a certain way become programmed into your mind. Your subconscious is conditioned, through repetition, by seeing or hearing certain things. Beliefs and behaviours can also be passed down through your DNA.

Many of the habitual ways you do things happen in autopilot mode. The subconscious mind is running the show, and you have little control over it. That is what makes it so difficult for us to change our habits. Oftentimes, we don't even realize we are doing the things we are doing.

I recently had a funny realization about a subconscious behaviour I've learned from my mom. I used to tease her for applying her lipstick in a certain way that made the stick wear down into a funny shape. As I was applying my lipstick last week, I realized I do the exact same thing. I'm not even aware of how I do it, but it is obviously a pattern that I subconsciously adopted from her.

Our Habits Control Our Lives

You have habits and beliefs (thoughts that you repeatedly think) that have been specifically ingrained in your subconscious mind through your past experiences as an employee that you might not even be aware of. To grow into your role as a business owner, you will need to recognize some of your habitual ways of thinking and acting in order to intentionally make shifts toward different ones.

In his book *Change Your Paradigm, Change Your Life: Flip the Switch NOW!* Bob Proctor explains the process necessary to change our behaviours. "It takes a change in paradigm, and a paradigm is a multitude of ideas that are fixed on our subconscious minds. Ideas that are fixed in our subconscious mind are known as *habits*. A habit is an idea that expresses itself without any conscious effort; you just automatically move."

The habit you need to change might be something simple like holding back from sharing your ideas in a group discussion, or it could be something more significant like thinking that you are not good at managing money, which can impact your ability to manage your finances effectively.

Let me share a practical business-related example. In your career, you may have been able to avoid doing some of the things you now need to do as a business owner. Or you may have formed beliefs about your ability to do something based on your experience as an employee. Let's say you know you will need to speak publicly to build your business, but you have a deeply rooted paradigm that you are a terrible public speaker. It may be because you received negative feedback from a former boss, or perhaps you have developed this paradigm because you compare yourself to the professional speakers you scroll past on social media. You tell yourself the story that you could never be as good as others. While holding onto this paradigm, the odds of you taking the actions to secure speaking engagements are very low.

Getting to the Root

The best way to alter your paradigm is to reprogram your subconscious mind to change a behaviour. This starts by becoming aware of your paradigms through self-reflection. Once you are aware of your paradigms, you can work on changing them from the root: your internal thinking. This will allow you to change your external actions.

The subconscious mind can only accept ideas and does not have the ability to reject ideas. One of the most effective ways to reprogram the subconscious mind is through frequent, spaced repetition of new thoughts infused with emotion.

If you want to change your paradigm about your speaking ability, you may choose to start repeating (in your mind and in writing) that you are a comfortable, confident, and engaging speaker who loves presenting. Through repeatedly telling yourself this new truth, you will begin to start feeling it as your truth. You can write it out over and over, then record yourself saying it and listen back to your voice repeatedly. Embody how you would feel if you were a comfortable and engaging speaker. This might sound silly or like a waste of time, but this is the most productive way to change a paradigm.

Over time, the belief on the inside will change and it will be expressed in the actions you take. You will slowly start to believe that you are a good speaker, and soon you will take the actions needed to secure speaking engagements. Or, even better, you may be presented with speaking opportunities—opportunities that you once might have turned down—and naturally say yes. It doesn't mean that you won't feel butterflies before you speak, but it does mean that you will be able to manage the nerves as excitement that you're about to do something new instead of experiencing anxiety or fear that you can't pull it off.

I don't want to make light of this process or present it as if it's easy and simple. It takes digging, along with openness and dedication to the process to uncover your deeply programmed beliefs. But for you to grow and expand, these are the necessary changes.

Energy Connects Everything

Now that we have a clearer picture of our mind, let's explore how energy works and how it relates to our minds.

We live in a universe made up of energy. Science has proven that everything in the universe is made up of atoms that vibrate at varying frequencies. From the chair you are sitting in to the tree growing outside your window, everything is energy vibrating at a certain frequency in a physical form. Therefore, everything in the world is made of the same energy but presents itself differently according to its vibrational frequency.

Universal energy flows into our minds and we use it to form thoughts. People have different names for this energy: source, spirit, consciousness, the universe, unseen force, or God. You can use whatever name you are most comfortable with. I will use universe for our conversation.

Our thoughts create a vibration in our bodies. Our feelings are our body's way of letting us know what vibration we are in. From these feelings, we take action through our bodies. When you think a thought like, "Here I go again, procrastinating on doing what I said I would do. I always do this," it creates a low vibration in the body, and you may experience feelings of sadness or anger.

When you think a thought like, "I love knowing that every day I'm getting closer to my goal," you vibrate at a higher frequency and will experience feelings like satisfaction and joy. Your thoughts, which you have the ability to choose, can alter how you feel in any situation.

So even though you may be down to the last few dollars in your bank account, you have a choice. You could think, "I'm broke, I don't have enough money," and you will experience feelings of despair and hopelessness. Or you could think, "I like the feeling of having more money. I like that I had enough to pay my rent this month. I appreciate the money I do have." Can you see how the latter thought creates a different energy in your body?

Your feelings are an indication of what vibration you are in. Your vibration matters because it impacts what you attract to yourself.

You Are Always Attracting

There are natural laws that govern how the universe works. You are likely already familiar with some of them, like the law of gravity, for example. You may have also heard about the Law of Attraction, which got a lot of attention when it was the subject of the movie *The Secret*.

The Law of Attraction presents the idea that you attract things into your reality that match the vibrations of your energy. Your mind is like a magnetic force attracting to itself. Your outer world reflects your inner world. When you are feeling good, you are putting out good energy and good things are attracted to you. Like attracts like.

Have you ever noticed that when something bad happens early in the day and puts you in a bad mood, one thing after another happens to make it worse? Or if you are having a great day, more good things just keep coming your way? That is the Law of Attraction at work.

Regardless of whether you believe it or not, you are always attracting things to yourself. To put it another way: what you focus on, you get more of. This is good news because it means that you can use the power of your mind to your advantage.

REFLECTIONS

What are your key takeaways from this chapter?

What new ideas will you commit to trying or implementing in your business?

Chapter 7

Follow the Breadcrumbs

I USED TO BELIEVE THAT THE ABILITY TO CREATE something or to achieve a goal was solely dependent on my ability to plan, work hard, and force and control it into being. I now understand there is another way. Yes, I still need to take action to reach my goals, but I now use my mind differently. I listen to my intuition and allow the universe to support me along the way. This approach has made me feel much more at ease and has profoundly shifted how I experience life.

I've gone from being a highly logical person trying to plan out every step of the way and control the outcome of everything to being more flexible and open to working with the universe. I now trust that everything unfolds exactly as it is meant to, even when it doesn't seem that way at the time.

Some of what I'm about to share may sound "out there," but I encourage you to stay with me. At one point, I was where you may be now. My highly logical mind fought hard for a time against believing some of the ideas to be true, but I've done a complete 180. I've integrated these concepts into my life and had unexplainable experiences which have led me to believe with absolute certainty that there is an unseen force working in the background of our lives.

Creation, Manifestation, Success…Whatever You Want to Call It

When we form an idea in our mind of something we desire or want to create, it exists as a thought. Everything in our physical world started as an idea in someone's mind. The universe responds to our thoughts and supports us in mysterious ways to help us turn our desires into reality. Some call this the process of manifestation.

To receive what we want in physical form, we must align our vibration with the frequency of what we want to attract, and then we must be open to receiving it. This is the Law of Attraction that we talked about earlier. When we stay in a natural state of feeling a sense of well-being, we receive ideas and impulses to do things.

By focusing on that which we desire, we give our mind direction to seek out ways to find it. Have you ever noticed how when you decide to buy a car of a certain make and model, you start seeing them everywhere? They have always been there; you were just not aware of them because you weren't looking for them. In the same way, by holding our desire in our mind, we start to become aware of how to bring it about.

The universe also guides us towards what we want through little signs and meaningful coincidences, otherwise known as synchronicities—those perfectly timed experiences that can't be explained with logic.

Have you ever felt an impulse to do something you couldn't explain, done it, and then bumped into the exact person you needed to meet? Have you received an opportunity to do something that has come to you through an odd set of circumstances? Or have you come across something that you somehow knew you were meant to see? These are the kinds of occurrences people respond to by saying, "Wow, what a coincidence!" This is the universe supporting the process of manifestation behind the scenes.

Here is one way that I have experienced this in my business. As 2020 was ending, I was thinking about what I would like to experience more of in my business in the coming year. I decided I would like to create a way to bring together things I loved to do into some sort of offering: reading and learning, facilitating, building community, and creating new things. I thought about how I would feel if I created something that stitched together all of these things. I decided I would feel excited and fulfilled. I practised generating those feelings through visualizations and connecting to those feelings in other areas of my life. This put me in a vibration to attract what I wanted, even without knowing what form it would take.

An idea came to me while I was walking one day: what if I created an online community for business owners to read business books together, and support each other in implementing what they have learned through a mastermind type of experience? It was only a spark of an idea, but it excited me, so I knew I was on the right track. The longer I held the idea in my mind, the more ideas came to me.

I focused on staying in a high (positive emotion) vibration and several unplanned circumstances unfolded that allowed me to create the whole program in just a few weeks. The structure for the program effortlessly flowed out of me onto a piece of paper, the name popped right into my head, and resources I needed to make it happen started to present themselves to me in a way that felt almost magical. Opportunities to promote it fell into my lap.

I launched the Business Book Collective in February of 2021 and quickly attracted twenty-four members who joined the community. I manifested, or brought into physical form, a program that matched my desire. I led a year-long program that was very fulfilling, and at the same time, created a new revenue stream for my business.

There was no feeling of controlling or forcing throughout the process, and this was quite the opposite of how I had approached projects in the past. The entire experience had an incredible feeling of *flow*. Yes, I took actions, but it felt like I was dancing with the universe as all the pieces of the puzzle fell into place so perfectly.

If this is a new concept for you, I know it may take some time to fully digest. As a recovering logically minded person, I found it very difficult to believe this "working with the universe" concept to be true. But as I've seen it play out in my own experiences over and over, I now fully accept it to be true.

Listening to the Whispers

According to Wikipedia, the word "intuition" is defined as "a thing that someone knows or considers likely from instinctive feeling rather than logic or conscious reasoning." In other words, every one of us has an internal guidance system—the little voice inside that whispers to us. Some call it your inner self, your higher self, or your inner being. Your intuition is the inner being that gives you gentle nudges to guide you towards what you want.

People experience intuition in different ways. For you, it could be an "inner knowing" about something you can't explain. A seemingly random idea might pop in your head, or you might be compelled to reach out to someone without understanding where the feeling came from.

You may feel a physical sensation in your body when something happens. Some refer to it as a "spidey sense" or "gut feeling." I feel tingles in the top of my head when my intuition is trying to get my attention.

The voice of your intuition is most clear when you are still and quiet with only your thoughts as company. In a world of information overload where we are perpetually busy, it's easy to lose touch with our intuition. Even something as simple as taking a few moments to close your eyes and breathe can help reconnect you to your intuition.

As a business owner, you will need to rely on information and data to make decisions. These are important, of course, but I also encourage you to pay special attention to your intuition. That little voice in your head or the feeling in the pit of your stomach is often trying to guide you down the right path and steer you in the best direction.

I had an experience in the early days of my business where I ignored my intuition—and then regretted ignoring it. I was referred to work with a client. From our first conversation, I had a spidey-sense that we were not going to be a good fit. On the surface, it looked like a good opportunity, but something about how he interacted with me in our first couple of meetings had my intuition buzzing.

I ignored my inner voice because I was thinking about the sizeable fees I would earn from the engagement. Boy, was that a mistake! The engagement turned out exactly how my inner voice had told me it would be. He was extremely difficult to engage and communicate with, and every phase of the project was a major struggle.

It's not always easy to follow your intuition. It takes courage to make decisions that might go against rational thought. But in my experience, intuition has always set me on the right path.

The Universe Leads the Way

Cora Tsouflidou, the founder of the successful chain of Cora Restaurants, tells the story of how she was recovering from a period of job burnout. She walked by a run-down building, on which was a "Restaurant for Sale" sign that caught her eye. Somehow, she knew there was something there for her:

"A miracle often occurs the moment we realize that by working relentlessly in pursuit of some ideal, we shut ourselves off from the forces of the universe at our disposal. When we neglect our balance, basic needs and a connection to a sustaining serenity, the ultimate architect of our lives brings us back to order. They make miracles happen as many times as needed until we finally get it. Without warning, and often without us realizing it, they send us brilliant ideas, prophetic dreams and magic keys. The greatest miracle that happened to me that day was that I believed in that Restaurant for Sale sign without wholly understanding what it was telling me."[2]

Looking back, I can see many synchronicities in my life that I didn't recognize as such at the time. When I resigned from my job, I planned to take the summer off to recharge and flesh out plans for my new business, which I hoped to launch in the fall. For a few weeks, I was in full-on recharge mode: going to yoga, taking long walks, and catching up on stuff around the house. I was feeling aligned and in flow. I was feeling carefree and excited about the possibilities ahead.

That's when the universe stepped in to speed up my timeline.

I got an unexpected phone call from a strategy consultant who had been a partner at the accounting firm I had worked for. He told me he was working with a client who needed help with marketing. They were a family business in the steel construction industry. My first two thoughts were, "What the heck do I know about marketing steel?" and "I'm not even in business yet!"

---

[2] Adapted from Mdme. Tsouflidou's Letter on Cora Restaurants Facebook Page on February 27, 2022, titled "Heal Yourself By Doing What You Love."

After some persuading, I agreed to have lunch with the president of the company, and we hit it off. I was open about the fact that I was new to the world of entrepreneurship. I described the need I thought existed and the type of business I was hoping to launch in the fall. At the end of what turned out to be a very long lunch, he turned to me and said, "Well, you have to start somewhere, so it may as well be with us. Send me a proposal."

That lunch led to the birth of Good to Grow Marketing, and a long-standing business relationship where I have done some of the most gratifying work of my career. That relationship also led to a network of other companies that became my clients.

I now see this experience as a beautiful synchronicity and example of the Law of Attraction in action. I had expressed a strong desire to start a business and was feeling aligned as I was recharging after leaving my job. I was open to possibilities, and the universe led me to an opportunity.

Here's what I want you to take away from this story: I didn't need to have the exact plan for my business laid out in detail. By holding an idea of what I wanted to create in my mind, staying open to possibilities, and following the breadcrumbs, I was led to the right person at just the right time.

Of course, there is a place for planning, but remember to also stay open to the magic of the universe guiding you along the way.

Start with Gratitude

One of the most powerful emotions you can actively cultivate is gratitude. Being in a state of gratitude and appreciation for what you already have creates a connection to the universal energy. You may have heard people suggest writing a gratitude list. The key is to not just write the list, but to also genuinely and deeply feel the sense of gratefulness that the words evoke in you.

In *The Science of Getting Rich* by Wallace D. Wattles, the author writes, "If it is a new thought to you that gratitude brings your whole mind into closer harmony with the creative energies of the universe, consider it well, and you will see that it is true."

Make a habit of writing a list of gratitude items every day and focus on really *feeling* grateful in the process. You can also use images or songs to access the feelings of gratitude and appreciation.

What You Focus on Will Grow

With an understanding of how energy works as well as the Law of Attraction, can you see why focusing on what you want is so important? And how important it is to focus on being grateful for all the things that you do have or have accomplished to attract even more good into your life?

When creating your business, you could think about all the things you have to do, all the things you don't know how to do, and how far you'll have to go to build the business you envision. Or you could choose to focus on appreciating every small step you take and enjoying the journey you are on. Holding thoughts that make you feel good will attract more good ideas, more people, and more resources.

Be sure to celebrate your small wins, along with each step of progression you make. A good practice is to keep a notebook on your desk, and every time you have a win—no matter how big or small it is—write it down. This will train your mind to look for more wins to create and celebrate. If you have a day where you feel frustrated or overwhelmed, review the pages in your journal to refocus your mind on what is working.

What are your key takeaways from this chapter?

What new ideas will you commit to trying or implementing in your business?

Chapter 8

Understand Your Hidden Superpower

ONE OF THE MOST CRITICAL THINGS I'VE LEARNED in my study of mindset is the power of our beliefs. They are your hidden superpower! The thoughts you repeatedly think form your beliefs. What you believe defines how you experience everything in your life, including the decisions you make and the results you get.

What you believe to be true becomes true for you.

Unfortunately, many of our beliefs are self-limiting ones based on stories we have constructed in our minds that block us from moving forward. The good news is that when we can see our self-limiting beliefs for what they really are—false self-limiting beliefs—we can deconstruct them and choose new beliefs to build. We can open new levels of possibility for ourselves.

If you were leading a team of people, you are only as strong as your weakest link. If one person was holding back the entire team, you'd fire them, right? You would probably go on to hire someone else who will hopefully propel you all forward. This is exactly how it works with your beliefs. You have a group, or team, of beliefs in your head, and you will only be as strong as the weakest one. You need to "fire" any beliefs that hold you back, and "hire" beliefs that will be valuable assets.

Believe for a moment that your business could fail based on statistics. Now, believe for a moment that your business is going to be successful and make a huge impact in the world. How did each belief feel? Which felt more empowering and motivating?

If you wake up every day believing that building your business is going to be hard, it is going to be hard. I do not wish to downplay the fact that a tremendous amount of effort will be required, but know this—the belief that you start off with will have a significant impact on what unfolds.

I urge you to be very aware of the beliefs you are holding. We all have the ability to choose our thoughts and beliefs in a way that supports our life. As you read on, I will share with you a few ways that your beliefs will have an impact on your business.

Build Your Belief in You

You need to believe in yourself and your abilities.

You can do anything that you believe you can, and that includes building a successful business. As Henry Ford said, "Whether you think you can or you think you can't—you're right." While you might not have evidence that this is true yet, start by looking at your past experiences.

Did you get a job that others said was beyond your reach? Did you overcome an illness? Did you bring an idea for something into reality? Did you show discipline and stick with something when most people would have thrown in the towel?

The truth is that you can do anything if you believe you can.

With every step you take in building your business, you will be creating more evidence of your ability to be successful. You will gain momentum, and your confidence will keep growing. Someone told me that once I had my first client under my belt, it would boost my confidence in my ability to build a business as a marketing consultant. It was true.

Sell to Yourself First

If you don't believe in your own abilities or what you are selling, nobody will buy from you. It doesn't matter if you are selling a sweatshirt or a business consultation. If you hold any negative beliefs or hesitation about the quality or value of your offering, it will affect your energy. This energy will come through in your marketing and sales conversations. Your lack of confidence will be felt by your customer, no matter how you try to cover it up. A buyer may have an uneasy feeling, or investors might not be willing to take a chance with you.

Think about a purchase you were hesitant to make. You needed to buy a new stove, and the salesperson helping you was very nice. However, as he explained about the stove, you noticed that he seemed to doubt the product. He trailed off weakly whenever mentioning the benefits of the stove, recoiled when you asked questions, and avoided eye contact. Were you sold? Were you ready to hand over your money and walk out glowing with excitement about your new stove? Probably not.

I recently had a conversation with a good friend who was selling spaces in a program. Her goal was to enroll six clients. She was doing all kinds of marketing, but nobody was signing up. She thought she had a marketing problem, but after digging deeper, I helped her see that her mindset was blocking her from attracting the right clients.

When she was honest with herself, she didn't feel comfortable with parts of the curriculum. Instead of adding more marketing activities, she made changes to the curriculum. The changes ultimately shifted her belief in the program, and wouldn't you know it, she soon signed up four clients.

Then she stalled again.

She went into push mode for the last two clients. With a desperate energy underpinning every action she took, she did everything she could think of. She couldn't decide if she would run the program with only four people. The indecision was leading her to feel anxious and unsettled, and this was the energy from which she was communicating.

Once she finally decided that she would run the program with only four clients, she felt like a weight had been lifted off her shoulders, and her entire perspective about the program changed. Surprise, surprise—the day before the program started, the last two clients signed up.

Build a product or service that you know in your heart will provide massive value for your clients or will enhance their lives in a meaningful way. Allow your genuine enthusiasm to shine through. You will be amazed at how that energy will attract the right people.

You Don't Need a Permission Slip

As women, we often hold the belief that we don't have enough authority or credibility. We don't believe we are experienced or qualified enough to go for things that men with far less experience or qualifications don't hesitate to put their hat in the ring for.

This belief shows itself when we believe we need to take another course or get another certification. While there is a time and place to pursue education and strengthen your skills, make sure that you do it with the right motivation.

Are you looking for a permission slip to do the thing that you know in your heart you are more than qualified to do? Do you feel like having that certificate will make you more worthy of bringing your expertise to the world? What if you decided to just start from where you are, with the underlying belief that you already have all the experience and wisdom needed inside of you?

ENTREPRENEUR INSIGHT

Powerful women in business are hyper-aware of the value they bring. Once women truly understand that their value comes from WHO they are vs. WHAT they do, a transformation begins to blossom internally. They are so well practised in how to feel full and therefore no longer feel the need to prove themselves to anyone. Once that happens, they start to feel in full command of their voices.

— Teresa Vozza, *Executive Coach*

Don't Put Yourself in the Box

Some women limit their belief in the possibilities and keep themselves in a box. I want you to consider this question: What do you believe about what is possible for you?

As a new business owner, you may feel inexperienced because you have never had a business. If you fixate on your lack of experience, you discount the wealth of expertise that you do possess and that you can bring to the world. This fixation can cause you to stifle your belief in what is possible and to keep your vision limited.

There will be a natural progression to the growth of your business, but don't get stuck in the mindset of restricting yourself from the most fully expressed version of the business you are creating. When you are spending time in your Visionary role, always continue to expand your thinking into all your business could become.

Build Beliefs to Support Yourself

How do we start building more self-supporting beliefs? The first step is to recognize when you are limiting yourself with a belief (often created based on a past experience or an assumption about what could happen). This awareness alone starts to open your mind to taking on a new belief.

I'd like to share a simple example to demonstrate how our beliefs affect our everyday actions. I was recently working with someone who needed to send an email to one of her clients inviting them to take an action. It was a very simple email, but every time I asked about it, she hadn't sent it.

She told me she wasn't sure if the language of the email was okay. I reviewed the three-line text, and it was fine. After some more probing, she shared that she got an angry response the last time she sent this client an email. She believed, based on this previous experience, that if she sent this client an email—any email—she would get another angry response. I helped her see that she was creating this story in her mind. She acknowledged what was happening and how it was holding her back, and finally let go of the belief that it would turn out badly. She sent the email and the client responded right away with a cheery note.

This may seem like a small, insignificant example. However, our beliefs hold us back from doing important things, from small actions like sending an email to making large, important decisions like going after a big client or increasing our prices.

The first step to shifting a belief is to decide on the belief you want to have. Beliefs are just thoughts we repeatedly think. They are often fictional stories that our minds hold onto, trying to keep us safe. We have the power to choose any belief.

Choose your new belief and set the intention in your mind that you are going to take on the new belief. If it is a small belief like in the example I shared, simply setting the intention to have a new belief can be enough to experience a shift and take action.

Other beliefs are larger and more deeply fixed in our minds, such as believing that you are only capable of earning a certain sum of money, or believing that you are not the kind of person who does this or that. Imagine how shifting a larger belief like "It's going to be hard to get clients" to "I'm easily attracting the clients I'm meant to work with" would support your mindset and impact the actions you take every day.

If you catch a belief that does not serve you beginning to come up, redirect your thoughts to the belief you're adopting and use repetition of the thought to cement it into your subconscious mind, much like we talked about doing with your self-image script.

In the next chapter, we will explore more practices and tools that will help strengthen your mindset.

REFLECTIONS

What are your key takeaways from this chapter?

What new ideas will you commit to trying or implementing in your business?

Chapter 9

Support Your Mindset

LEARNING TO WORK WITH YOUR MINDSET is not something you figure out how to do in one day. It is a continual process of expanding your understanding and learning. You can incorporate practices into your day that will help your mind and your energy stay in flow.

Manage the Cranky Voice in Your Head

Most people would not speak to other people the way they speak internally to themselves. The talk track playing in your mind throughout the day happens automatically based on your habitual thinking. In *The Untethered Soul: The Journey Beyond Yourself* by Michael Singer, the author uses the analogy of the continuous internal chatter being your "inner roommate," and compares the roommate to a "disturbed, annoying, and emotionally reactive person."

As the leader of your business, you need to be your own biggest fan. You need to be ruthless about shifting that voice to be one that supports you. That voice is your thoughts, and you control your thoughts. Your thoughts then dictate your feelings, and those feelings influence your actions.

Start by paying close attention to when the voice comes up, and softly shift to a better-feeling thought. Instead of thinking, "I have no idea how to do this and I'm never going to figure it out," you could reach for a better feeling and more supportive thought like, "Okay, I've never done this before, but I'm just going to take it one step at a time, and I know I'm going to be able to do it."

Use Perspective to Shape the Situation

There are many angles from which any situation can be viewed. You can view situations in a way that causes you stress and anxiety and provides evidence for the negative story you've been telling yourself. Or you can choose to view situations in a different, more positive angle, and watch a better story unfold.

Let's say you launch a new program, and your goal is to have twenty-five people join in. Only fifteen people enroll. You could tell yourself that you failed to reach your goal, beat yourself up, and create negative energy around the whole program.

Or you can choose to say to yourself, "Yeah!! Fifteen perfect people enrolled in my program, and it is going to be an incredible experience for them. I'm going to learn so much working with this group and deliver an amazing experience for each person who joined. I'm going to take the lessons to apply for my next group, which is going to be even bigger because of the positive reviews these fifteen people are going to provide. At the end of the day, this is my first cohort and I have years of running this program ahead."

Doesn't that feel much better? Whenever you find yourself feeling low when thinking about a situation, remember that you hold the power to shift your perspective.

Quiet Your Mind

I've been an off-and-on meditator for many years, but didn't establish a routine until a few years ago. Meditation has become a regular habit that I find very supportive.

Meditation is the best way to quiet the inner chatter of your mind and tune in to your inner guidance. I start and end almost every day with a meditation session that is usually between fifteen and thirty minutes.

You may be saying to yourself, "I don't have time to meditate!" I'll counter your argument with what the Dalai Lama always said: "If you don't think you have time to meditate, it's time to meditate."

If you are new to meditation, don't be intimidated. Keep it simple. When I meditate, I sit quietly on a chair with my eyes closed and focus on a small sound in the room or repeat a word like "release" in my mind silently. If I notice my mind starting to wander, I focus back on the sound or the word. It's that simple.

When I am meditating, sometimes a thought will pop into my mind and give me an answer to something I've been thinking about. Sometimes I'll receive a thought or idea that seems quite random. I mentally note it and then decide if I should follow the breadcrumb. When I do, it often leads me to something interesting or helpful in a way I wouldn't have expected. Other times, I just enjoy the feeling of peace, and come out of the meditation feeling calm and centred.

Some people prefer to start by using guided meditations in which someone verbally walks you through a session. Choose a style that works for you and build a habit of regular meditation.

Engage Your Imagination

Everything that has been created in the world was created in the mind first using the imagination. Our mind thinks in pictures, so using your imagination can help to bring something from a mental picture into reality in the world.

Visualizing your goal, the successful business you have built, is a healthy practice to engage in every day. Let your mind paint the picture of what you are creating. Connect to your emotions and feel the feelings you'll experience and the impact you'll have once you reach your goal. This will help magnetize yourself to attract your vision to you.

I suggest getting into the habit of building a five-minute visualization session into your day. Do it as a part of your morning routine to get yourself fired up.

Put Pen to Paper

I love a beautiful journal. I used to have a stack of pretty journals with a few pages of randomly captured thoughts in them. I later learned how to journal in a way that was helpful, and I now have a stack of journals that are full on each page. I realize that when I thought I was journaling before, I was really only creating Dear Diary entries. I was documenting things that happened rather than exploring ideas.

Our minds are designed to seek out answers to questions. With journaling, you can use writing to pull answers out of your-self or clarify things that you are feeling uncertain about. Getting your thoughts on paper can lead to breakthroughs you wouldn't reach otherwise.

I often start by writing a question at the top of the page and take a few deep breaths to connect to my intuition. I might write something like, "Is this business opportunity right for me at this time?" or "What is the best next step on this project?" or "Why am I feeling this way?" Then I start writing. I just let the ink flow freely, and I don't judge or edit anything that comes out.

Sometimes it is a slow start, and sometimes it comes quickly. In almost every case, the answer I am looking for becomes clear. Thoughts that I wasn't even aware I was thinking flow from my pen. New ideas arise. Solutions suddenly become obvious.

I encourage you to experiment with journaling.

Associate Feelings with Objects

One way to be intentional in your thinking is to use an object (e.g., a piece of jewelry) or a visual of a certain word (e.g., "Empower"). Having these in your environment can act as visual triggers to remind you to be intentional in your thinking.

Sharon Gilmour-Glover, Co-Founder of Light Core Inc., provides a beautiful example of how she uses objects to support her mindset as she navigates health challenges. "When I go to chemotherapy, I put on a jade Buddha a friend gave that helps me stay grounded and I wear a beautiful bracelet made especially for me by my friend's daughter to help support my healing. Putting these objects on reminds me to tap into my internal, personal energy. It reminds me to anchor to times I have felt strong and at my best. Wearing this jewelry doesn't change reality. I still have chemo. But it changes the energy I bring into the session. My medical team has told me countless times that my positive attitude contributes directly to my physical health."

I have a bracelet that belonged to my grandmother that I wear to remind myself of my feminine power. I use my engagement ring, which I wear every day, as a reminder of my abundance. And I have a "Believe" sign on my desk that acts as a reminder to believe in the universe's power to support me.

What objects can you bring into your world that will trigger the feelings you want to experience in creating your business?

Think from Your Future Self

My daughter Stella is the master of using this mindset hack. When she doesn't want to do something, she asks herself, "How would future Stella feel if I did this now?" The answer is almost always, "She would be happy that present Stella sucked it up and did it." Okay, here's the truth: sometimes she does say, "That is a problem for future Stella," when she really doesn't want to unload the dishwasher.

There are going to be things you need to do in your business that will make you feel uncomfortable. Reminding yourself of how you'll feel once you have completed the task can help you move into action. When you are making decisions, think from the place of your future self. What would the person you created in your self-image script do in the situation?

What are your key takeaways from this chapter?

What new ideas will you commit to trying or implementing in your business?

Chapter 10

Know There Is Only One You

AS YOU SET OUT ON A PATH TO BRING YOUR SERVICE or product to market, you may be filled with excitement about the prospect of helping someone solve a problem. Then, you may see someone else offering a similar service, and your enthusiasm takes a nosedive. Does this sound familiar?

In this chapter, I want to help you understand who you really are and share some perspectives on how to think about competition in a healthy way.

Let me start by reminding you that you are the only person in the world who has your unique blend of wisdom, skills, and experience. The lens through which you see the world is unique to you. The way you'll deliver your offering to help your clients will also be unique to you.

When you think about it that way, you are not really competing with anyone, are you? Nobody can "do you" in the way that you do. You are creating what you are intended to bring to the world, and so are they. While you may be serving the same market, different people will be attracted to different businesses. Understanding this concept can be very freeing as it helps you to stay focused on what you are creating and not become distracted or disheartened by what other people are doing.

It's also important to remember that people are buying more than the product or service you are selling. They are buying the transformation you help them achieve, which we will talk more about in an upcoming chapter. They are also responding to your energy and how you make them feel. As Maya Angelou shared, "I've learned that people will forget what you said, people will forget what you did, but people will never forget how you made them feel."

ENTREPRENEUR INSIGHT

At the beginning, I did not see myself as a business owner, period. I saw myself as a freelancer. This freelancer mindset made me feel like I was in the back seat, with less power in how or where things could go. I simply saw myself as selling my work. Now, I better understand my value, which goes beyond the tangible work that I produce, and encompasses my own spirit in everything I create. THAT is what clients hire me for.

— Reina Takahashi, *Paper Artist*

Competition Is a Good Sign

Undoubtedly, there will be other companies that provide solutions to your customers' challenges. When you are starting to research other companies, you may start feeling concerned that there are too many other companies offering something like what you are offering, and that the market may be saturated.

The fact that other companies are successfully serving the market is a good sign! It is a demonstration of the need for your offering, and that people are willing to invest their money in finding a solution to the problem you are helping to solve.

Stay in Your Lane

Managing your mental energy to stay focused on what you are creating is crucial. One of the best ways to support yourself is to control what you allow into your experience.

Social media can be a great source of research, but it can also throw you off your focus. One of the fastest ways to spiral into a puddle of self-doubt is to give in to the urge to pick up your phone and start scrolling social media. I'm sure you understand how easy it is to get sucked into the never-ending feed and lose an hour. But what you might not fully appreciate is how what you're viewing is impacting your mental state.

Following the feeds of more established companies can help in your learning process and can generate inspiration. But if you find yourself shifting from becoming inspired to comparing yourself to these companies, it's time to put the phone down.

Someone shared a great analogy with me that compared building a business to running a marathon. They said that you must get comfortable with people passing you. Don't look back at the people behind you or at the people way ahead of you, as doing so will be a waste of your valuable energy. Stay in your lane, stick to your plan, and keep putting one foot in front of the other.

Celebrate Your Competitors

We have been taught that competition is the enemy. We are in a battle against the competition to win the customer. There is a winner and a loser, and we are all fighting for a piece of the pie with a limited number of pieces.

This type of thinking is based on a scarcity mindset that leads to making comparisons to the competition. It creates a sense of lack, rather than the feeling of abundance that comes from focusing on creating.

This may sound counterintuitive, but hear me out. What if you instead took on the belief that there are more than enough people for both you and your competitors to serve? What if you believed that you are all trying to collectively solve a problem that exists for your collective customers?

With that view, wouldn't you want to celebrate your competitors when you see them being successful?

Send your competitors gratitude for helping the people they are meant to help, knowing that you too will help the people you are meant to help. Then get back to creating what you're meant to create.

What are your key takeaways from this chapter?

What new ideas will you commit to trying or implementing in your business?

PART 3

Create Good Habits for Self and Business Management

THRIVING COMES FROM HAVING a strong foundation of habits, routines, and systems in place that support you. In this section, we will talk about the importance of building your community, as well as the mental shifts you should be prepared to make as you step into your new world.

I'll share some suggestions, which are often habits, to stay focused and get things done, along with practices to sustain your energy. We will also talk about approaches you can take to maximize your impact in everything you do. We will finish by exploring your money mindset and building good habits around managing your finances.

Many of the things you'll read about may seem unimportant, but it is the small and seemingly insignificant habits that build momentum over time. In *Atomic Habits: An Easy & Proven Way to Build Good Habits & Break Bad Ones* by James Clear, the author defines what he calls an "atomic habit" as the following: "a regular practice or routine that is not only small and easy to do but is also the source of incredible power; a component of the system of compound growth."

Clear suggests adopting the practice of *habit stacking*, meaning to "identify a current habit you already do each day and then stack your new behavior on top."[3] For example, I have created a habit stack where I meditate for fifteen to thirty minutes as soon as I wake up. The established behaviour is waking up, and the newly stacked behaviour is meditation. It now happens on autopilot. As you're reviewing this section, think about how you can use habit stacking.

[3] https://jamesclear.com/habit-stacking

Chapter 11

You're Not in Kansas Anymore

WHEN DOROTHY FOUND HERSELF IN THE Land of Oz in the movie *The Wizard of Oz*, she quickly realized she was not in Kansas anymore. She was in a different world, a world where she would discover many new lessons on her journey back home. Stepping into self-employment, you may feel a bit like Dorothy—out of place, confused, and not sure where you are. Let's focus on some of the mental shifts and related habits that will support you as you step into your new Land of Oz.

Take Initiative

Nothing happens in your business unless you initiate it. If you are used to being more of a direction taker than a direction maker, you'll need to adjust your approach to be more proactive. Direction takers make great employees, but not great business owners.

Taking initiative can mean anything from planning your activities to picking up the phone to call someone to spark a conversation. Start by taking on small tasks that will move you forward. For example, if you feel hesitant to reach out to people because you're concerned that you'll be bugging them, here is a simple mindset shift that I find very helpful: Always think about what you can do for the other person in return for what you're requesting. It could be something as simple as offering to introduce them to someone in your network or promoting their business to show your support. When you're offering something first, it feels easier to make an ask.

Taking action is what helps our confidence grow. The more we initiate and take action, the more evidence we create in our minds of our own capabilities.

Keep Planting Seeds

In the early days of your business, it may seem like the amount of work is disproportionate to the result you get from it. You may be networking and writing blogs and speaking at events, but little appears to be coming from your efforts. This can feel discouraging. Your mind may try to play tricks on you by creating a story about what it all means. Be mindful of the narrative your mind is creating, and remember you have the ability to choose your thoughts. Keep pulling your focus back to the vision of what you're creating.

Every effort that you make is planting the seeds for your future success. Sometimes it takes time for those seeds to gestate. We can't control the time of gestation. We can only hold our focus on what we want and keep focusing on the part we can control: taking action.

Start with Something, Not Everything

As an entrepreneur, you'll always be scanning the landscape and listening for problems that need to be solved, and hopefully coming up with solutions. Remember, rarely does anyone get it all right out of the gate, so don't worry about thinking you have to.

Being an entrepreneur is about bringing new ideas, products, and services to market, getting feedback, and continually refining and adapting your plans and ideas as you go. It's important to keep an open mind and not get stuck in your preconceived ideas of the way you thought things would be. Keep the end goal in mind, but be open to the form it takes.

Rather than investing excessive amounts of time and money in the initial phase of launching an offering, a good approach is to pilot ideas and develop a "minimum viable product." This means you launch a basic version of your offering and continue developing and refining it based on real customer feedback.

For example, you may plan to launch an online course that will be pre-recorded for clients to go through at their own pace. Before investing all the time and energy into building the full course and recording all the lessons, you could start by running a live version of the course with a small group. You can get it into the market quickly, generate some revenue, and apply the lessons you learn to the pre-recorded program.

ENTREPRENEUR INSIGHT

Get your product or service into the market before you think you are ready. The market will tell you what it wants. You can't sit in your office refining and refining until you think it is perfect. Let the market tell you; and the market tells you with dollars. You need to bring in dollars. Otherwise, you don't have a business, you have a hobby.

— Jen Kelly, *CEO and Founder, New Initiatives Marketing*

If you remain open and flexible, you'll shape your business and offerings in the way that is best for your clients.

ENTREPRENEUR INSIGHT

It Doesn't Have to Be Perfect Out of the Gate

When I decided to leave the corporate world to start my financial education and consulting business, I thought I had to have it all perfect upfront and I wasted a lot of time and money at the beginning. I invested in research I didn't need and spent more time building things than I needed to, rather than getting them out into the world.

I now understand that you don't have to do it all out of the gate—create your minimal viable offer, get traction, get feedback, and then build from there. Four years later, I have 500+ women from all over the world in my Strictly Money online financial program building financial confidence and wealth, and I have launched a national personal finance TV show to advocate for Canadians' financial wellness.

— Saijal Patel, *TV Host, Strictly Money & Financial Wellness Educator & Consultant*

Strengthen Your Decision-Making Muscle

One entrepreneur I interviewed shared this great insight: "The best part of being an entrepreneur is making your own decisions. The worst part of being an entrepreneur is that you have to make your own decisions."

Building your muscle for decision-making is a critical skill. If you routinely avoid making decisions, you'll waste time and mental energy. You will have your own decision-making style, and the ability to be self-reliant and make decisions quickly and confidently is a skill that will serve you well.

When you stop for a minute to tune into your intuition, you often know the right decision. It's when you start second-guessing yourself and asking for everyone else's opinions that you create a problem. Of course, there are cases when it's a good idea to ask for advice from someone who has the right experience or knowledge, but most decisions don't require a committee of opinions.

To strengthen your decision-making skills, start practising with small decisions in your life. When you're at a restaurant, scan the menu, decide what you want, and close the menu. Decision made. When you receive an email with a question that you'd typically mull over, decide quickly, and respond immediately. Decision made. By practising on the small things, you will start training your mind to be more comfortable when making bigger decisions.

Everything That Happens Is Feedback

As an entrepreneur, it's easy to take setbacks personally because your business depends on you and is intertwined with your self-identity.

I used to be very quick to judge myself when things did not turn out to be the way I thought they should. I was quick to beat myself up for what I identified as failures. Those stories of failures can pile up in our minds and affect our self-confidence and ability to move forward. I now have a different perspective on failure that feels so much better: everything that happens, including failure, is feedback.

A great quote by Price Pritchett in *You2* says, "If you send a rocket toward the moon, about 90% of the time it's off course. It fails its way to the moon by continually making mistakes and correcting them."

When something doesn't go as planned, try to separate yourself from it. Treat it as feedback that you can learn from, and then make the necessary changes accordingly. It is not always easy, but it's a much more productive and self-supportive approach that will help you keep going.

There are also times when something doesn't work out and the lessons are revealed further down the road. You can only connect the dots when looking back, so when facing a challenge, always keep a little curiosity in the back of your mind about the lesson or connection that will someday be revealed from it. Remember, there is an unseen force at work beyond what we can always understand in the moment. We need to have faith that things unfold exactly as they are meant to and trust the timing in our lives.

As an example, a few years ago I launched a program for entrepreneurs. In my mind it "failed" because I didn't attract any interest from potential clients. Looking back now, I can see the reason the venture failed was more related to my lack of belief in myself. I now realize that the program's content was fine, but I ultimately did not believe that I was qualified to deliver it.

Here's the connection I couldn't have seen then. The content from the program informed much of the content for this book. As I write this book now, several years later, I have more experience and a different mindset supporting me. The time and effort I invested in developing that program was not wasted. It wasn't a failure. It was preparing me for where I am today. I just couldn't have known it then.

BUSINESS INSIGHT

Be a Goldfish

I am in love with a television show called *Ted Lasso*. In the show, Ted Lasso, an American football coach, is unexpectedly recruited to coach an English Premier League team, despite having no experience in European football (soccer).

In one scene, one of his players makes a mistake during a game, and Ted can see that it is affecting him. Lasso calls the player off the field to try to snap him out of it.

"What's the happiest animal in the world?" asks Lasso.

The player says he has no idea.

"Goldfish," Lasso replies. "You know why the goldfish is the happiest animal on earth?"

The player has no clue.

"Got a ten-second memory," answers Lasso. "Be a goldfish."

If you make a mistake in your business or something doesn't go as planned, it can be debilitating if you stay stuck in the story of your failure. Don't let what has happened in the past take control of your future. Take the lessons and move on. Be a goldfish.

Watch the Stories You Tell Yourself

There are times when you'll hear no, often in the beginning. A client will choose to work with someone else. Your idea will not be accepted. The person you're reaching out to for help will decline.

No is just a word, but there is danger in hearing it repeatedly because you could create a story about what it means about you. If you allow rejection to affect your self-worth, it can damage your mindset. Permitting thoughts like "I guess I'm not good enough or smart enough" can quickly cause you to spiral into a dark place.

When you face rejection, treat yourself with kindness and focus on learning from the experience. Catch yourself if the negative thoughts start to creep in—then redirect your thinking. Remind yourself that everything happens for a reason. Not getting that client could have saved you from a nightmare working situation! Think about the lessons you can take away from anything that could be perceived as a failure. Is there something you can do differently next time?

Embrace the Suck

Building a business will require you to do things you have never done before. You'll need to expand your skills into new areas. In your employee life, you probably felt pretty good at your job and comfortable in most aspects of your role. You may have participated in professional development to grow your skills, but it was often related to areas specific to your role.

Finding yourself suddenly in a world where you must figure out how to do things that you've never done before can feel daunting and humbling. It can also be frustrating if you're a person who is uncomfortable with learning new skills. If you're used to being good at things right out of the gate, it can be hard to accept that you don't know everything. You need to be open to learning.

Adopting a growth or learning mindset can support you as you try new things. With a growth mindset, you believe your knowledge and talents can be developed over time. I love the advice

Brendon Burchard, the world's leading performance coach, offers: "Embrace the suck, and do it anyway." In military terminology, to "embrace the suck" simply means to have discipline.

Your first blog post is probably going to suck. Your first video is probably going to suck. Your first discovery call is probably going to suck. That's okay! It's all about practising and developing over time. You just need to start. Put your ego aside, be open to learning, and have patience with the process and yourself.

For many years, I avoided using video in my marketing because I was terrified of being on camera. I held the belief that I just wasn't good at it. I finally reached a point where I realized I could no longer avoid using video, so I signed up to participate in a thirty-day challenge to go live every day on social media.

The first few days were painful. I spent a long time learning how to use the camera and making sure I looked good. I rehearsed exactly what I was going to say. I looked like a deer in the headlights in my first video, obviously uncomfortable and stumbling through my words. A few videos later, they were a bit better. By the end of the thirty days, I was going live without any makeup and sharing conversationally instead of relying on a script. Who was this person??

Not only did I get more comfortable making videos, but I discovered that I actually enjoyed it! Now I use video regularly in my business. If I hadn't been open to embracing the suck and continuing to film myself day after day, I never would have been able to develop that skill.

Decide in your mind that you will learn the new skill. Keep showing up and supporting yourself by giving yourself grace along the way.

Make Fear Your Friend

Sometimes we can mistake fear as a sign that we are heading in the wrong direction. However, fear can actually be an indication that we are heading in the right direction. Fear can also arise when we are stretching beyond our comfort zone and on the verge of growing to a new level.

Barbara Stanny interviewed successful, high-earning women for her book *Sacred Success*. She shared that, to her surprise, every seemingly confident and successful woman she interviewed admitted they had struggled with fear and self-doubt at some point. They felt fear and moved forward anyway.

Fear is simply something we construct using our own imagination. If you can use your mind to imagine fear, you can also use your mind to imagine the opposite feeling: courage.

This concept clicked for me a few years before I left the corporate world. I was in the audience for a live taping of *The Oprah Winfrey Show*. Her guest that day was Tony Robbins, a world-renowned motivational speaker. The topic of the show was "Overcoming Your Fears." It was as if Tony was talking directly to me.

He talked about how the fictional stories we make up in our minds—about the way things are or could be—hold us back. He talked about how many of our fears were created from childhood experiences, and how ridiculous it is to let a story we created in our seven-year-old mind run the show in adulthood.

I listened intently to every word. At the end of the show, he came over to the edge of the stage and shook my hand. I should more accurately say, he shook my arm with his massive hand. I felt a surge of power when our hands connected.

In that moment, I realized all the fears I was feeling about starting a business were being constructed in my mind. If I created them, I could let them go. It was the first time I started to understand the power that my mind has over my experiences. And I realized how stepping through what we fear most can take us towards what we want most.

You're very likely to come up against fears in your entrepreneurial journey. Before stepping away, ask yourself if stepping into the fear is actually the right next move.

REFLECTIONS

What are your key takeaways from this chapter?

What new ideas will you commit to trying or implementing in your business?

Chapter 12

Find Your People

HAVING YOUR OWN BUSINESS CAN BE VERY rewarding, and it certainly has its bonuses. But there will be days when you'll feel like you're swimming alone in an ocean, missing the safety net of having coworkers. You will miss having people around to socialize with and to bounce ideas off of. You'll also miss having access to people with different talents to rely on. It can feel lonely. That's why it's vital to intentionally surround yourself with people who will support and inspire you.

Don't Try to Fly Solo

Friends, family, and former colleagues will have the best of intentions to support you, but they are not always the best people to turn to. If they do not have experience with entrepreneurship themselves, it will be difficult for them to offer meaningful advice, as they cannot truly understand what you're going through.

One of your priorities should be to start building a network of people who run their own businesses. You will learn from their experiences and perspectives, and these relationships can open up opportunities with potential clients and vendors. Developing a strong network can also give you a view of how other people are doing things, which you can then extrapolate from and apply to your own business. Being in the energy of a community can help you gain momentum more easily than if you try to go it alone.

ENTREPRENEUR INSIGHT

Finding a community of business owners that I could talk with was key for me. All the insecurities when I looked out and saw everyone else "crushing it" were really challenging until I met some great-hearted entrepreneurs that I was able to share honestly and vulnerably with. Suddenly I didn't feel alone. I knew we were all in the same struggle and the beauty came through knowing if we worked together in support and collaboration, we could help raise each other up. Instagram won't give you that gold. A great support community and mentors will.

— Jennifer McCarthy, *Owner of Bluhouse Market and Café*

You can start by looking for people in your own network to connect with or asking friends if they know of anyone to introduce you to. There are many in-person and online networking groups you can join to find your people. Be clear about your reasons for joining each network, and limit yourself to joining only a few specific groups initially so that you do not spread yourself too thin.

As your business evolves, you will need different types of support. When I first started my business, I joined a women's networking group that I knew would help me gain confidence and meet potential vendors. At some point, I felt like I had outgrown that organization and decided to join a different peer-to-peer advisory board consisting of more established business owners. This new group provided more individual support tailored more specifically to my needs.

Leverage the Power of Multiple Minds

If you're interested in a more structured method for engaging with other like-minded business owners, you might also consider joining a mastermind group. I am a member of two mastermind groups that meet regularly to support each other.

A mastermind group is a peer-to-peer mentoring group. Members help each other solve their problems by providing input and giving advice. The concept was coined by author Napoleon Hill in his book *Think and Grow Rich*.

Hill defined a mastermind group as two or more people coming together in harmony to solve problems. The intention of a mastermind group is to leverage the power of multiple minds coming together focused on the same goal—goals like growing your business. In a traditional mastermind group, each member can share advice or ask for feedback through a very intentional and structured format.

Keep Yourself on Track

It can be easy to let yourself off the hook when you don't have a boss to answer to. It's important to have methods for motivating yourself and holding yourself accountable to do what you say you're going to do.

A great way to do this is to have an accountability partner with whom you share your commitments and check in with regularly. It could be another business owner you met through a networking group or a friend you know will hold you to your word. I have an accountability partner I send a Marco Polo video chat to every day. I share what I'm planning to work on and update her on where I'm at with my previous commitments.

We keep each other on track, support each other, and lovingly call each other out if we are not staying true to our intended focus. No one knows you better than yourself. If you're the kind of person who is most effective when you have someone else to answer to when it comes to goals and deadlines, I would highly recommend finding an accountability partner.

Connect with Actual People

I don't miss my former commute, but sometimes I miss having colleagues around for casual pop-in conversations and quick chats while grabbing a coffee. You can easily feel isolated if you don't make a point of reaching out to people. We all need human connection.

It's important to get out from behind your desk and connect with real people! Each week, get in the habit of looking ahead at your schedule and plan to attend a few face-to-face meetings or networking events. Remember, connecting doesn't always have to be in person. Make a habit of scheduling a virtual coffee with someone in your network once a week. The more people you connect with, the more you'll learn and the more potential opportunities you will uncover.

Co-working spaces are also a great way to put yourself in an environment where you can meet other business owners, often with complementary businesses. Being surrounded by other people can feel uplifting and provide opportunities to make connections. Even if it is only for one or two days a week, it can be a nice way to break up your routine and get energized by a fresh environment.

Invest in Yourself to Save Time, Money, and Energy

Finding a mentor or coach who has experience in building the kind of business you're building can be valuable. While your business will be unique, you don't have to reinvent the wheel. By seeing what others have done, you can extrapolate lessons, shape them into your own, and apply them to your business.

I remember people talking about investing in business coaches in my early days of business and thinking, "I can't afford to hire a coach. That seems like a waste of money. What could they really do for me anyways? I'm smart, and I'm determined to figure out what I need to know."

Having since invested in working with a few different coaches, I now understand the value of hiring one. With an outside perspective, coaches are able to ask you questions to guide you in the right direction and keep you focused. They can help you see blind spots and identify gaps in your knowledge. They will accelerate your learning by sharing their own experience. And perhaps most importantly, they will call you out on your BS, and push you outside of your comfort zone.

ENTREPRENEUR INSIGHT

Get advice at the start. Whether it is for accounting, a business coach, or a mentor, even if you think you can't afford it. It will pay for itself in no time.

— Cathy Landolt, *Founder, Blue Elephant Productions*

It may sound counterintuitive to invest in a coach or learning program before you have clients or revenue, but it can dramatically speed up your learning curve and save you frustration and money by making better-informed decisions upfront.

There is also something energetically significant about being willing to invest in yourself. If you're not willing to invest in yourself or think you don't have enough money to invest in developing new skills, you will attract clients with the same mindset. Remember, like attracts like.

REFLECTIONS

What are your key takeaways from this chapter?

What new ideas will you commit to trying or implementing in your business?

Chapter 13

Stay Focused

I CLEARLY REMEMBER DAY ONE OF MY FIRST JOB after university. A small accounting firm hired me for a newly created marketing role. I was excited about the job, but at the same time, I was nervous about taking on the role with so little experience. I was hoping the partner I was reporting to would provide me with some direction.

I arrived at the company and was shown to my office by my boss. The sparsely furnished room had a desk, a computer, and a blank notepad with a pen sitting on it. He said, "Okay. Well, here you are. Have at it." I was literally given a blank page and no guidance. At first, I was terrified, not knowing where to begin or what to do. But soon, I became excited about the opportunity I had been given to create something by starting fresh—to create something out of nothing.

This is much like the beginning of your journey into self-employment. You have a blank page, and you can create the business you want. Nothing happens until you decide what needs to be done and start doing it.

Someone once told me that in the beginning, self-employment can look a lot like unemployment. This is true. As an employee, your days are structured and probably involved a lot of meetings.

Other people's schedules largely dictated your time, and you likely had a boss who assigned your work.

As an entrepreneur, your days are wide open for you to start filling with activities. If you don't develop a disciplined approach for how to stay focused and spend your time, you can easily find yourself wasting days without achieving much.

If you're working from home for the first time, this freedom can present challenges if you're the kind of person who is easily distracted. There is always another load of laundry to do or dishes in the sink, or a Netflix show calling you.

Discover What Works Best for You

We all have the same amount of time in the day. It's what we do with this time that matters.

Earl Nightingale, one of the original thought leaders in personal development and the author of *The Strangest Secret* said, "Time can't be managed. I merely manage activities. Each night, I write down on a sheet of paper a list of the things I have to accomplish the next day. And when I wake up…I do them."

Creating supportive habits and being intentional about how you plan your activities is the secret weapon. If you don't own your day, your day will own you.

There is no single method or golden rule on how to best manage your focus and activities. You need to figure out what works best to motivate yourself and facilitate your best productivity. The following sections will present some approaches that have worked for me and other successful entrepreneurs.

Create a Dedicated and Inspiring Workspace

For the first few months of running my business, I was operating from the kitchen table or a corner in our bedroom. I was constantly shifting my workspace around. As a result, I felt scattered and found myself becoming distracted by things around the house. I figured out very quickly that this approach wasn't going to work for me.

At some point, someone made an off-handed joke about me moving into the shed. The joke sparked an idea, and before I knew it, my very handy husband was converting our tiny shed into a fully insulated, heated, and air-conditioned office that is now my own. It's small, but it's perfect. I have a space that is my own and gives me a quiet and inspiring place to work every day.

While you might not be able to create a separate office, it's important to create a dedicated space that allows you to be focused. Having a space you specifically associate with work helps you switch your mindset to work mode. Our environment can also have an impact on our energy. When you're in a space that makes you feel good, it helps raise your vibration.

If you're interested in learning more about creating a "she shed" or "cloffice" as they are now being called, you can check out this blog where I shared some tips: www.goodtogrowmarketing.ca/good-to-grow-blog/what-ive-learned-about-working-from-the-shed

Make Planning a Habit

It's easy to get caught up in busywork and not make progress on the things you need to do to move your business forward.

Set monthly goals, and then spend time planning out your priority goals for the week. Break down the tasks you will accomplish each day. Be realistic about what you can accomplish in a certain period of time and leave yourself some buffer time for unexpected things that come up.

I try to identify three things I must get done each day and then some nice-to-have goals. I find it helpful to take some time at the end of Friday to begin planning for the following week. This way, when Monday comes, all the week's next steps are top of mind.

Use whatever system works best for you. If you like to plan digitally, use project management software. If you prefer paper, a good old-fashioned day planner works. We'll talk more about options for project management software in Chapter 15.

Break It Down

David Allen's book *Getting Things Done: The Art of Stress-Free Productivity* presents a system for "stress-free productivity." Two key concepts from the book are very helpful when prioritizing your work.

The first is to "capture" a task in its entirety, then break it down into sub-tasks. This helps to break a large, daunting task down into smaller, more manageable ones. To use writing a book as an example: you would have to come up with an outline, write the content, work with an editor, design the cover and layout, and upload the book on Amazon. Each of those steps is a sub-task of writing a book.

The second key concept is "next action." When planning your time, review the list of all the sub-tasks and decide what the "next action" is to achieve your goal and focus only on accomplishing that task. Instead of worrying about all the steps that need to happen, focus only on the next thing needed to move the project forward.

This approach can be incredibly helpful when working on a large, complex project or deciding which areas to focus on when you're managing multiple clients or projects at once.

Don't Get Too Excited about Checking the Boxes

I recently came across the term "completion bias" and it really hit home. I read about it in an article[4] that talked about research being

---

[4] https://lifehacker.com/beware-of-completion-bias-when-working-through-your t-1766677655

conducted by Harvard Business School. The research focused on how people approach tasks.

The article shared the following: "Human brains are wired to seek completion and the pleasure it brings." It continued, "Our ongoing research (not yet published) has found that checking off items is psychologically rewarding. After you complete a task, being able to literally check a box makes you happier than when you are not given a box to check."

This may sound positive, but the dark side of completion bias happens when we are more motivated by ticking off boxes than by prioritizing the most meaningful tasks. As someone who loves making my way through a good checklist, I've been guilty of aiming for more checked boxes.

Make a habit of prioritizing the most important or creative work, which is not necessarily the most urgent work. I like to tackle this work first thing in the morning while I am fresh. I use ticking off the smaller tasks as a reward later in the day. This approach will help you to make progress on meaningful work first and not get sucked into the busywork.

What Gets Scheduled Gets Done

If you look at my Google calendar, it will appear that my days are fully booked. That is because I schedule my day with blocks of time dedicated to specific tasks I've identified for the week. I block the first hour of each morning for "goal-achieving activities" (which are dedicated to accomplishing three tasks that will move me towards whatever my priority goal is) or for "deep work" tasks. That may be a "working on the business" task or a specific project like completing an assessment for a client, or in my case, writing this book.

Deep work, as described in *Deep Work: Rules for Focused Success in a Distracted World* by Cal Newport, is a critical element for thriving. He defines deep work as "focused, uninterrupted, undistracted work on a task that pushes your cognitive abilities to their limit." Schedule time for regular deep work in your week.

Another reason I like time blocking is because it creates self-imposed time limits to get things done. Have you ever noticed how if you give yourself three hours to get something done, it takes three hours? But if you have only one hour to get the same task done before heading out for an appointment, you get head-down focused, and it somehow gets done? Using time constraints can make you more productive.

Don't Be So Stubborn You Sabotage Yourself

What I am now going to share might seem like a contradiction to what we just talked about. While it's helpful to schedule your time, you also need to pay attention to your energy when approaching the task. If you approach a task with the wrong energy, you won't be effective. Instead, you'll drain yourself by trying to will your way through it.

Let's say you have blocked time to record a video first thing in the morning, but you wake up feeling physically and emotionally depleted for whatever reason. You have a choice to make. Should you be rigid and go ahead with recording the video because it's what you said you would do? Or would it be smart to tend to yourself first, shift your energy, and record the video later?

How do you think the session will go if you try to force yourself? You're more likely to struggle through it. Even if you do get dressed up and smile, your energy will come through in the video. The result is not likely to be good, and you certainly won't feel good about it.

Instead, think about re-arranging your day to focus on doing work that doesn't require the same high energy but can still move you towards your goal. Do something supportive for yourself that will help to raise your vibration. Something as simple as taking a walk or having a little dance party in your kitchen can start to shift your energy.

Minimize Distractions

We live in a world of continual distractions. A continual flow of social media notifications, emails, phone calls, and all the other distractions of working from a home office. Jumping around between tasks can have a big impact on your productivity.

Two of the biggest distractions are your smartphone and your inbox. I suggest keeping your phone on silent during your focused work sessions, and only checking your inbox during specific points in the day rather than checking in constantly. Social media can be extremely distracting and can trigger feelings of anxiety. I've removed the Facebook and LinkedIn apps from my phone as I found myself spending too much time scrolling and didn't like the way it was making me feel. This simple move has opened time for more useful activities and made a big difference in my ability to stay focused.

BUSINESS INSIGHT

Stay Focused on What You Need Right Now

Seeing an endless list of sponsored posts for the latest course on the topics of "Facebook Advertising" or "Growing Your List" does nothing but evoke two very unproductive feelings: panic and self-doubt.

Panic comes when you start reading about random topics and begin to think, "Oh no, I should be doing that!" Self-doubt creeps in when you think, "Wow, this guy knows so much, and how the heck is he doing X when I can barely get through managing the admin of my business, finding new clients, and then actually delivering the work! I must not be cut out for this."

This is one of my own go-to thought spirals, and I can validate how debilitating this type of thinking can be. I now recognize that these thought patterns often come up when I feel tired and depleted. If you catch your inner voice going down a dark road, recognize it for what it is, and shut it down.

If there is a specific resource you need, you'll be able to find it when you need to access the information. Stay focused on *your* plan for developing *your* business and servicing *your* clients. Shut the rest out.

Bring Intention to Everything You Do

The intention you bring to anything you do will change how you experience both the process and the outcome. When you focus your mental energy on something while holding an intention, you give your mind a specific direction.

When you spent your days going between meetings, you walked into each meeting room with a specific intention in mind for that meeting. While you no longer have meeting rooms to go between, you can mentally create segments to your day.

Treat each thing you do as a segment—or "meeting"—in your day and approach each thing with intention. When you sit down to work on a project, close your eyes for a few seconds and think about what your intention is for the task. How do you want to feel working on it, and what do you intend to achieve?

Getting in the habit of taking a simple pause to set your intention is a great practice. It helps to increase your effectiveness and reset your energy as you move between a variety of experiences that require you to show up in different ways.

Batch and Combine

Creating the habit of grouping together similar activities can be an effective strategy. Examples are blocking times for entering expenses, responding to new client inquiries, or creating social media content.

Creating social media content is one area where batching can be a real benefit. Batching content allows you to get into the mindset of creation and into the flow of writing. Create multiple posts in one time block and pre-schedule them using social media scheduling software. This will take the pressure off creating and posting content on the fly.

Create Start and End Times

Without the requirement of showing up to an office at a specific time, your start time can easily get delayed. Likewise, it's just as easy to lose track of time and continue working into the evening, long after you would have "clocked out." When you're passionate about your business, you can feel compelled to just keep working and working, which can be unhealthy over time.

Creating boundaries is an important method for delineating between your work and personal life. Using rituals and routines can help transition from the workday to the evening. It may mean planning your next day, closing your computer and taking a walk, or doing fifteen minutes of meditation to reset your energy for the evening.

BUSINESS INSIGHT

Give Yourself Grace for a Change of Pace

While it's important to establish your new routine, I also want to remind you to give yourself some grace in the early days as you adjust to your new lifestyle.

The pace of work may feel different from your previous world if you lived with hectic deadlines in a high-stress environment. Some days you may feel like you're not doing much. On those days, give yourself credit for every little action you take towards building your business, because they all add up.

On other days, you'll feel like a mad scientist, fueled by passion and excitement, wanting to work around the clock. Remember to pace yourself. There is a risk of having your passion turn into an unhealthy obsession that can lead to burnout.

In the Harvard Business Review article "What Makes Entrepreneurs Burn Out,"[5] the authors reference a study conducted to determine which factors lead to greater burnout among entrepreneurs. They stated, "Some evidence suggests that entrepreneurs are more at risk of burnout because they tend to be extremely passionate about work and more socially isolated, have limited safety nets, and operate in high uncertainty."

The findings concluded, "Entrepreneurs who reported high scores of obsessive passion were more likely to say they experienced burnout than those who reported high scores of harmonious passion." Harmonious passion was defined as being "motivated by the job because it brings them satisfaction and is an important

---

[5] https://hbr.org/2018/04/what-makes-entrepreneurs-burn-out

part of who they are," with obsessive passion meaning "the job is important to someone because of the status, money, or other rewards that it brings."

Remember that building a business is not a sprint; it is a marathon.

It's important to have open communication with people in your life. If you have a partner or family, talk to them about the adjustments you're making. Some days it may look like you are not doing much, and they may be concerned. On other days, they will be asking if you are still a part of the family because you seem to be missing in action and at your desk for endless hours.

I've found that sharing what I'm up to with my family helps them understand the ebbs and flows in my world, and saves everyone a lot of frustration.

Not Every Idea Needs to Be Executed

As an entrepreneur with the freedom to do whatever you want, you'll see new ideas, opportunities, and shiny objects everywhere! When you're full of passion, you want to solve all the world's problems! But if you pursue every idea that comes to you, you'll quickly find yourself spread too thin and veering off from accomplishing your clear vision.

When something new comes into your world, ask yourself, "Is this going to help me move towards the vision I have?" If the answer is yes, then decide if it is the right time to pursue it and if you have the bandwidth to take it on. If not, park it until the time is right. If the answer is no, spend some time refocusing on your vision.

REFLECTIONS

What are your key takeaways from this chapter?

What new ideas will you commit to trying or implementing in your business?

Chapter 14

Keep Your Battery Charged

BUILDING A BUSINESS REQUIRES SUSTAINED ENERGY. Your health, wellness, and vitality are critical to showing up and doing the work. Learning to generate, protect, and manage your energy is just as important as your other business-related responsibilities.

Much like a battery, you need to keep your mental and physical energy charged to keep yourself from becoming depleted. When depleted, you can't show up as your best self and you increase your chances of getting sick. You also create the perfect environment for the cranky roommate in your head to start ramping up negative thoughts of self-doubt.

Take it from someone who has had to learn this lesson over and over. I was so depleted at one point that I ended up in the emergency room being assessed for a potential heart attack. That experience was a real wake-up call about how depletion can show up in our bodies.

Well-being is the foundation of everything. Nothing matters more than your health. Period.

Wellness Comes First

I'm not going to get into specifics around nutrition or exercise. You need to find what is right for you. Having a solid approach to maintaining your health includes doing all the things we know we should be doing. Preparing nutritious meals, exercising, and getting quality sleep. Prioritizing your health helps to optimize your energy and the attitude you bring to the day. It can also provide an insurance policy by keeping your immune system strong, so you don't get sick and have to take time away from your business.

One of the most effective habits I've created to support my health is pre-planning dinners for the week and preparing food on Sundays. I know that when I get busy, one of the first things to slip is my healthy diet, like it is for many people. I grab something quick that is not necessarily fuelling me effectively, or I forget to eat altogether. When I'm not eating well, I notice almost immediately how it affects my energy levels.

When I've prepared some freshly cut veggies and batch-cooked and portioned out some soups and salads for the week, it makes having a nutritious lunch much easier. As the primary cook in our household, pre-planning dinners also helps me transition into the evening and helps my mind feel more settled when I'm able to answer the dreaded question, "What's for dinner?" It becomes one less distraction taking up valuable space in my mind.

Find the best ways to fuel your body with the nutrition, movement, and sleep that works best for you. When you feel your best, you can bring the best of yourself to your business and your clients.

Feed Your Mind

How you start your day can determine how the rest of it will go.

Do you roll out of bed, grab your phone immediately, and start scrolling social media or news headlines? What you feed your mind first thing in the morning will set the tone for the rest of your day.

A better approach is to start your day intentionally with uplifting activities to boost your mood and feed your mind. Creating a cluster of small habits or a morning routine can make a huge difference in how you feel. Give some thought to the habits you could adopt to start your day off right. Here's a look inside my morning routine.

BUSINESS INSIGHT

A Solid Morning Routine to Start the Day Right

This is how I start my day. I get up between 5:00 and 5:30 am and kick off my morning routine. I meditate, write a list of things I am grateful for, journal, and study mindset work. These quiet moments are my sacred alone time to think, plan, and dream while everyone else is still asleep. This is when I set my intention for how I am going to show up for the day.

Then I have a cup of coffee with my husband, and we talk about the day ahead. I love this time because it helps us stay connected. I then head out for a walk, either with a friend or while listening to a podcast or music from my "good feels" playlist. Music is one of my favourite ways to raise my vibration.

Next, I do a quick house tidy-up, make a green smoothie (you can find my smoothie recipe at www.goodtogrowmarketing.ca/bookresources), have a shower, and get dressed. When I walk into my office, I use walking through the doorframe as a trigger to shift my mindset into work mode. I say out loud (yes, this is a bit embarrassing to admit), "Good morning, Good to Grow Marketing. Let's do this." I sit down at my desk to start my workday.

This routine works for me and helps me start my day feeling positive and energized. It doesn't always happen exactly as planned, but I try to stick to my routine or incorporate a few of the elements if I'm short on time. On the days I'm not able to, I can feel it in how my day unfolds.

Something different might work for you. The key is having a way to start the day that sets you on the right track. Give some thought to what your ideal morning would look like. Experiment with a variety of ideas for as long as you need to.

P.S. Full disclosure, I have teenage children. Life didn't look like this when they were younger! Your morning routine will reflect your stage of life and circumstances. It might mean taking only five minutes to meditate when you sit up in bed, or thinking of five things you are grateful for. Even something this simple can make a huge difference.

I also suggest getting dressed to start the day—even if you're working from home. The clothes you choose to wear can affect your energy. Think about how you feel when you take the time to shower and put on a blouse and a pair of nice jeans compared to when you throw on some leggings and a sweatshirt. Think about how you naturally hold your body in each outfit. In which outfit do you feel more confident and energized? Getting dressed can also create a "work mode" trigger for your mind.

Take Breaks for Peak Performance

As a business owner, you will find an endless list of things that need to be done. The innate desire to serve your clients can drive you to just keep working and lose track of time. You need to pace yourself and take on reasonable periods of work, balanced by breaks to replenish your energy.

Like a race car driver takes pit stops to tune up their car so it continues working optimally during a race, you need to create little energy reset pit stops to optimize your energy. If you wait until your energy is already depleted to take a break, like a race car driver that passes the pit stop, you're more likely to run out of fuel … or crash.

Working constantly is of no service to your clients or yourself. Making a conscious effort to build the habit of taking regular breaks throughout the day is important. According to High Performance Coach Brendon Burchard in his book *High Performance Habits: How Extraordinary People Become That Way*, the world's largest study of productivity found that the most productive people tended to take a break every fifty-two minutes.

Beyond around fifty minutes, your brain has a difficult time continuing to focus. Set a timer to take a short break about every fifty minutes. Get up from your desk, grab a drink of water, do a quick stretch, and take some deep breaths. Even short breaks can help sustain your focus and energy.

Also build in some longer break times throughout the day to support yourself. I know a business owner who takes thirty minutes of her daily lunch break for whatever she feels like doing. It might be going for a short walk to get some fresh air, reading, or doing a guided meditation.

Avoid Two Killer Energy Drains

When I'm having a day where my energy is feeling low, I ask myself two questions:

"Have I been sitting for too long?"

"Have I had enough water?"

If you're working from a home office, you won't have the outside influences that naturally cause you to stand up from your desk. There are no interruptions from coworkers, meeting rooms to walk between, and lunch spots to walk to outside the office. Consequently, you're likely to spend way too much time sitting. Your body is designed to move!

Much like we talked about creating the habit of taking regular breaks, also try to incorporate standing time into your day. I recently purchased a stand-up desk that can quickly adjust between sitting and standing so I can easily alternate positions. I am amazed at how much this affects my energy.

The second energy drain to be aware of is dehydration. Without enough water, your brain function slows and doesn't work properly. You'll start to feel lethargic, and your cognitive ability will decrease significantly.

A little trick I use is to fill three large water bottles or mason jars in the morning and put them on my desk. I know that by the end of the day I must finish them. Having pre-measured water on my desk creates a visual reminder and it's easier to keep track of how much water I am drinking. If you are refilling the same glass or bottle before it's empty, you may think you're drinking more than you really are.

Manage What You Allow into Your Mind

Everything that comes into your mind can affect how you feel, and how you feel will ultimately affect the actions you take. That includes the conversations you have, the news you consume, the music you listen to, and the social media feeds you follow.

I am very conscious of what I allow into my mind. I have curated my social media feeds with content that makes me feel good. I try to limit how much I check the news. All these things help me keep my energy and mindset in check. You may argue that you need to watch the news to stay up-to-date or check your competitor's feeds every day to stay on top of what they are doing. I'd like to encourage you to think about how those activities make you feel. Do you feel nourished and energized after engaging in those activities, or do you feel drained?

If you feel drained, you may want to reconsider what you're allowing into your mind. During the early days of the COVID-19 pandemic, like most people, I was continually consuming the news. It was all changing so fast, and it was all so scary. It was taking over all my mind space and I couldn't concentrate on my business.

I realized I needed to take a different approach. I decided that the news that needs to find me, will find me. Yes, I still checked at times, but much less frequently. I immediately recognized the shift it created in my energy. I felt more optimistic and was able to focus. With my renewed focus, I was able to spend time working on rebranding my business and launching a whole new program.

Stay away from whatever drains your energy and flips you into a pessimistic place. Your friend might have the best of intentions by telling you about the number of businesses that fail, but is this really helping your mindset? Following certain people on social media might seem like a good idea, but if it makes you feel bad about yourself, hit mute.

Protect your energy and how you feel at all times.

Plan Your Work around Your Energy, Not Your Energy around Your Work

Everyone has a time when they typically feel most able to focus. Some people find they have their greatest energy first thing in the morning, while others are night owls. The key is to start observing your patterns to plan your work around your energy levels.

I used to schedule meetings first thing in the morning thinking I would get my meetings done and then dive into my to-do list. Over time, I discovered that the first few hours of the day are when my ability to focus is at its highest, and this is when my most thoughtful or creative work gets done. I now schedule meetings for after lunch whenever possible.

ENTREPRENEUR INSIGHT

Work with Your Own Energy Rhythm

One of the things I had to learn was to identify when I was at my peak for doing my most expansive, creative, and goal-achieving work. For me, it's between 9 and 11 am and I now protect those hours.

I know my mindset and how I am feeling affect my work, so I've developed practices to get myself to a better feeling place before I sit down to produce certain kinds of work. I also understand the importance of rest and taking breaks to sustain my energy, so I build downtimes into my day.

— Catherine Wright, *Sleep Coach, Educator and Speaker, Recoop*

Fill Your Cup

One of the reasons you probably want to start a business of your own is to have more freedom and flexibility with your time. Your goal is to not only create a business, but to also create a life you love to live. Don't forget to make time for the living part. It's easy to forget to live when you're in the throes of creating your business.

It's normalized in our society of hustle culture to accept and celebrate living in a state of depletion, but it does not have to be that way. You can choose to enjoy your life and thrive.

Schedule time to play or do the things that spark joy for you. Treat those times as you would any other appointment. Do what feels nourishing for you and helps you raise your vibration. It might mean going for a run, painting, taking a fitness or yoga class, or having lunch with a friend.

Here is the real challenge: schedule those activities into your day, and don't feel guilty that you're not working! The whole point of taking time for yourself is to help raise your vibration—to actually enjoy the life you've created! If you feel guilty the whole time, you're missing the point. Taking part in activities that enhance your sense of well-being helps keep you feeling aligned and magnetizes you to attract more into your life.

I used to have the equation backwards, believing that activities I classified as self-care were to be used as a reward for achieving a goal. I would push my way to a goal, often at the expense of my health, and then reward myself with some form of self-care, like a massage. This trap in thinking is what leads to burnout. To stay in an energy of thriving, I now build in self-care practices as a part of my process in achieving a goal. I double down during times I know I am going to be busy.

Thriving is a feeling you create within yourself. You deserve to feel good. It is not something you have to earn.

Spend Time Being, Not Doing

This is a lesson that has taken me a long time to learn, and I'm still working on it. I've spent most of my life filling every minute of my day with tasks and associating my self-worth with my level of productivity.

Does that sound familiar? I've now learned this is not the best approach.

It's critical that we spend time in *doing* energy to move forward towards our goals. We also need to spend time in *being* energy to allow ourselves to receive ideas and inspiration.

As an employee, you spend a lot of energy in *doing* mode because that is what is rewarded. The energy of *doing* triggers our sympathetic nervous system, the function of which is to stimulate the body's fight or flight response. This energy is what drives us, but it can be depleting to our bodies if we spend too much time in it.

When we are in our *being* energy, we draw on qualities like intuition, creativity, and collaboration. Tapping into our *being* energy can feel unnatural, but it can be the source of incredible power. This energy triggers our parasympathetic nervous system, which is that place of rest and digest that is regenerative for our bodies. If we spend too much time in *being* energy, we won't take action to move forward.

Neither energy is good or bad, and both serve an important purpose. Both *being* and *doing* energies need to be accessed at different times. When we are appropriately tapping into both energies and dancing between them, this is when our bodies are working optimally; this is when we feel like we are living in flow and thriving.

One of your energies will tend to be more dominant, and it is helpful to be aware of which you naturally draw on. Many business owners spend most of their time in *doing* in a way that feels forceful and leads to burnout. When we're excessively drawing on our *doing* energy working towards a goal, we can unintentionally block the access to our intuition and creativity.

By slowing down to just *being* and not *doing*, you can soothe your nervous system and tap into new ideas and creative solutions.

"Pushers have a fear-based belief that if they're not super productive, nothing will happen for them. Little do they know that their pushy energy is blocking their capacity to attract! The Universe doesn't respond well to frantic energy. Rather, the Universe vibrates at a positive frequency, and to co-create with it, your energy must align with that frequency," shared Gabby Bernstein in *Super Attractor: Methods for Manifesting a Life beyond Your Wildest Dreams*.

This may sound counterintuitive, but I've experienced the power of slowing down to find answers and creative solutions. I remember feeling frustrated trying to come up with a solution to a challenge. I was trying to think and act my way to a solution. I was feeling anxious and tense in my body. I reached out to my mindset coach for advice, thinking she would suggest a journaling exercise.

Instead, to my surprise, she told me to take a bath and put on a funny movie. In truth, at the time, I was a little annoyed because I couldn't comprehend how that advice could help resolve my problem. But as a good student, I listened. Wouldn't you know it— it worked! As I was brushing my teeth at the end of the evening, the answer I had been looking for came to me. It was so obvious that I couldn't believe I hadn't seen it before.

Slow down, take time to just *be*, and in *being* you might be surprised at how much easier life, and your business, seem to flow.

REFLECTIONS

What are your key takeaways from this chapter?

What new ideas will you commit to trying or implementing in your business?

Chapter 15

Become a Master of Effectiveness

WHEN YOU'RE AN ENTREPRENEUR, THERE ARE a million things to do: contracts, accounting, marketing, delivering work ... the list goes on. But being a business owner doesn't mean you have to do it all alone. You'll need to rely on other people and resources to get things done.

In this chapter, we will talk about some approaches that will help you stay focused and save time so you can become as efficient and effective as possible.

Focus on Your Sweet Spot

Even if it's just you in the business initially, it can be a mistake to try to do everything on your own. This mistake can affect you in two important areas: profitability and mindset. To the greatest extent possible, you need to focus your time on working in your "zone of genius" or "sweet spot," meaning the place where you add the most value for your clients, earn the most profit, and get the most satisfaction.

This is also where your time is best spent when it comes to driving your profitability. Tasks that drain your energy should be given to someone else. This may mean hiring a bookkeeper or a part-time virtual assistant so you can focus on your most impactful work.

Let's be realistic. In the early days, you will be doing everything on your own. However, from the beginning, it's important to be thinking about what tasks you can establish a process for and eventually delegate to someone else. For example, maybe you love writing and can write a blog post in thirty minutes, but get bogged down for hours finding and uploading a photo and sharing your post on social media. This might be something you identify as a task that can be easily outsourced in the future, so that you can focus on the part that you love—writing the blog.

Many entrepreneurs wait too long to bring on help because they think they can do it all themselves. Or they don't see the value in paying for the help. When you feel that you could use the help but are trying to push through a little longer, it is probably the right time to bring on some help.

Don't make the mistake of thinking that all people are seeking full-time jobs, or that hiring help in some areas will cost a lot. You may be thinking that it would be great if you could have help for a few hours a week for some tasks that aren't in your zone of genius. There is very likely someone out there who would love that job!

ENTREPRENEUR INSIGHT

Support Can Come in Different Shapes and Sizes

I put off hiring a virtual assistant for years because I thought that I couldn't afford to hire someone. Then I started to think differently about how I might be able to get support.

I needed help developing content for my blog and sharing it through social media and creating my newsletter on a regular basis. I knew this was important to establishing myself as a thought leader and staying top of mind with potential clients, but I never seemed to be able to get to it. When I did, I often wasted time fiddling with images and posting.

I reached out to a friend who had been a rock star in the corporate world and was now starting her own business. I knew she did a good job with her posts and could likely get me organized. I asked if she would be interested in working for a few hours a week to support my content creation and sharing. She was thrilled to have a role that she could fit into her life and provide a bit of extra income.

Fast forward six months and I now consistently create content that is being shared through my social media platforms. I engage regularly with my network and have received several inquiries from potential clients. The small investment I make has had an exponential impact on my business.

— Jennifer Schrafft, *Executive Leadership Coach, Jennifer Schrafft Coaching and Consulting*

There is a community of affordable support available: freelancers, virtual assistants, and outsourced solution providers through platforms like Freelancer, Fiverr, and Upwork. I had no idea that these resources were available to me when I first started my business.

I use these platforms to outsource various small projects and administrative tasks so I can focus on doing my most genius work. From doing layouts for eBooks to doing research to consulting on setting up a client management system—I've hired people from all over the world to do lots of jobs for me.

The other option is to hire a part-time "virtual assistant," also referred to as a VA, who regularly supports various administrative tasks. There are many types of VAs, with some providing general administrative help and some specializing in specific areas like social media support.

Let Processes Set You Free

You may feel like processes constrain you, but I believe they can set you free—free to consistently deliver a great customer experience and free to use your valuable time to work on the things that light you up.

When you're first starting your business, it's the perfect time to create and capture some core processes and develop good habits related to operating your business. This will save you time and allow you to more smoothly delegate tasks to other people over time.

I'm not talking about creating a library of complex Standard Operating Procedures that sits on a shelf. You just need to develop some simple steps to getting things done, along with the templates that will support you, and capture them in a way that makes them easy to share.

A good way to start identifying core processes is to recognize when you're doing a task that is repeatable. Next, think about whether you could capture the process, and eventually, have someone else do it. Then get in the habit of capturing the process.

Develop Your Core Processes

In Mike Michalowicz's book *Clockwork: Design Your Business to Run Itself*, he shares a framework I find very helpful in identifying the core processes to develop in your business. He calls this framework the ACDC model.

Michalowicz shares that every business exchange goes through a flow of steps, and that you can build processes or systems to save time and effort within each of these steps. Every business must do the following:

1. Attract

2. Convert

3. Deliver

4. Collect

I personally like to add a fifth category: Administration.

For each of these steps, let's explore some of the core processes to consider creating. I've used examples that apply to a service-based business. If you offer a product, think about the steps that your customers go through and what processes could be captured.

1. Attract - bringing in new prospects
   - Process for social media content creation, scheduling, and sharing
   - Process for posting content to your blog
   - Process for editing videos to add to your branding
   - System for creating email marketing content and schedule

2. Convert - turning prospects into customers
   - Standard marketing materials and accompanying scripts to be shared
   - Commonly asked questions and answers to be referenced in the sales process
   - Customizable proposal template
   - Engagement letter or client contract template to be customized

3. Deliver - supply the service (or product) you offer
    - Onboarding process for new clients
    - Customizable report template
    - Customizable client update report template
    - Offboarding process for clients

4. Collect - ensure that your fees are collected in return for your service
    - Customizable invoice template
    - Standardized monthly financial review and report

5. Administration
    - Standardized folder structure for storing files
    - Standardized project plan steps documented

Capture Your Core Processes in Simple Ways

Don't get overwhelmed by the idea of creating a long list of systems and capturing them all on day one, or even week one! Over time, you can develop your systems and capture them one at a time as they are executed. This way, you'll slowly build a library of resources to draw on.

Michalowicz also suggests a brilliant way to capture your systems. Instead of thinking through a process and documenting the steps in a written document, a process that is very time-consuming and often ineffective, leverage the power of video capture.

As you're about to complete a process, turn on a screen recording software and talk through each of the steps you are taking as you work on the screen. I use a free software called Loom that allows me to capture videos and store them in folders labelled with each of the ACDC steps. You could also store the videos in a file management system like Dropbox, making them easy to share with others.

Once the video is recorded, you can reference it yourself, or share it to delegate the task. If something changes in the process, you can re-record the video. Or ask the person using the video to re-record it if *they* recognize an update that should be made.

ENTREPRENEUR INSIGHT

Spend Your Time and Money Wisely

The two lessons that had the most impact on my business are the following: First, you have limited time every day, week, month, and year. You can't create more time. What you can create more of is money. Spend your time and money wisely. You think you will be saving money by trying to DIY everything, but this just ends up costing you your time, which is a finite resource.

Second, hire team members before you need them. Hiring help creates capacity, and this will accelerate your growth and with a lot less pain than waiting until you're past your capacity to hire help.

— Cynthia Mason, *Founder and Managing Lawyer,*
Mason PC Trademarks

Find Software to Support You

There are many different software packages to support every step of your client process. Everything from client management software to track your contacts, to appointment scheduling software, to social media management software.

Before deciding to invest in any software, be sure your business truly has a need for it and evaluate whether it's the right time for you to invest. Many software platforms take a lot of time and effort to get up and running, which can distract you from doing more important work in your business.

Be clear on what you need immediately, and then build out your software support structure over time.

ENTREPRENEUR INSIGHT

Before investing in any technology or software, be clear about what you need. As soon as the social media algorithms peg you as an entrepreneur, you'll be bombarded with ads for all kinds of software products that the company claims you must have to be able to run a successful business. It's easy to get sucked in. Many software platforms have overlapping functionality and if you invest before you're clear on your needs, you could end up wasting time and money on systems you don't really need.

— Valerie DuRoss, *Co-Founder, Crafted Communications*

Become a Master at Project Management

One of the not-so-sexy but key skills you'll need to develop as a business owner is project management. There are a few keys to effectively managing projects:

- **Get everyone on the same page at the beginning.** This includes defining the scope of the project and setting expectations of the outcome so that everyone is clear. This helps to avoid misunderstandings down the road.

- **Break down the project into a series of tasks with a related timeline.** Draw on using some of the habits we've already talked about, specifically those having to do with breaking down larger projects into smaller tasks.

- **Invest in project management software.** While I do suggest being thoughtful about which software to adopt in the early days of your business, a project management tool should be one of your first considerations. It's hard to stay on top of everything. I use Asana and love it. There are other great options like Monday and Trello.

- **Communicate—and often.** One of the main causes I see for projects going off the rails is a lack of communication. Be sure to communicate regularly about progress and bring any issues to the client's attention as early as possible.

Make it Easier or Make it Unnecessary

To close out this chapter, I would like to share a helpful concept from *The ONE Thing: The Surprisingly Simple Truth Behind Extraordinary Results* by Gary Keller. The author encourages readers to continually ask themselves a simple question. This question can be particularly helpful when you find yourself facing inaction because you feel overwhelmed and don't know where to start. He asks, "What's the ONE thing you can do such that by doing it everything else will be easier or unnecessary?" Rosie's story provides a good example of how taking one action had an impact on several areas of her business.

ENTREPRENEUR INSIGHT

Around the holidays, I was overwhelmed with inquiries about booking online baking classes with many people asking the same questions. I decided to create an autoresponder that would go out for every email I received. I created a short but cleverly worded email saying I was busy getting ready for the holidays in the kitchen. It included answers to a few commonly asked questions, a link to sign up for upcoming classes, and a link to download a free "Holiday Cookie Swap Party Hosting Guide."

This one simple action significantly reduced the time I spent responding to emails, increased sign-ups for classes, and added more people to my mailing list. Creating this one simple email made my life easier and helped me grow my business.

— Rosie Coelho, *Owner, Rosie's Kitchen Co.*

REFLECTIONS

What are your key takeaways from this chapter?

What new ideas will you commit to trying or implementing in your business?

Chapter 16

Keep Your Financial House in Order

THIS CHAPTER WILL TALK A BIT ABOUT YOUR mindset around money and appropriately valuing your offering. We will then focus on the practical matters of creating good habits and systems around managing your finances. When tax season rolls around, you'll be happy you did!

Check Your Money Mindset

Money is a fascinating topic to talk about as it relates to mindset. We all hold beliefs or paradigms that impact our relationship with money, both in our ability to attract it and our ability to keep it.

Many people have limiting beliefs about money. Our money beliefs are shaped through our upbringing and our life experiences. The ideas that become programmed in our subconscious mind, often at a very young age, affect our relationship with money.

Maybe you grew up hearing things like …

"Money is the root of all evil."
"You must work hard to make a lot of money."
"Money doesn't grow on trees."
"Rich people are not good people."

Can you see how holding these kinds of beliefs can cause you to self-sabotage and focus on lack? The truth is that money is not good or bad, but we attach stories to what money means for ourselves.

I encourage you to take some time to explore your beliefs about money. Start noticing the ways in which you habitually think about money. Pay attention to how you talk about money to other people. Notice what thoughts are triggered when you see people with money.

To shift to a more empowering money mindset, direct your attention to what you want. We know that what we focus on grows. Since we know this to be true, we should focus on feeling abundant in order to draw more abundance to ourselves. Nurture your relationship with money and become comfortable with the idea of having it. Welcome it into your life.

In the early days of your business, it can be easy to focus on the lack of money coming in which can put you in a low vibration. A great practice is to focus on the abundance you already have in your life. Abundance comes not only in the form of money, but in various blessings. This realization will put you in the vibration of abundance, and you will magnetize yourself to attract more abundance.

Focusing on lack can also show itself in different ways in your business, with one area being how you value your offering and price your product or service.

BUSINESS INSIGHT

Own Your Value

There are several options to consider when setting your price including the cost of creating and delivering your offer, the margin, and what competitors or similar businesses are charging.

Your financial goal will likely revolve around matching or out-earning your previous income. You can choose from several options to price your offering including a flat price, an hourly rate, a project fee, a retainer fee, or a membership or subscription-based offering.

Regardless of the route you choose to go, be careful not to underprice your services, which women often do. Yes, you are a new business owner, but don't forget about the value you bring based on the combination of your natural abilities and your previous experience. Price your services to reflect that value. Your pricing should feel like a bit of a stretch for you, but not so much that it causes extreme internal tension. Otherwise, you'll create the wrong kind of energy around your pricing.

It's important to keep in mind that not all people buy services the way you do. What you're proposing to charge may feel higher than what you may be willing to spend yourself, but remember that you may not be your ideal client. If you have a solution that will help your client save time and money or achieve a specific outcome, they will be happy to pay.

ENTREPRENEUR INSIGHT

Someone has to be the most expensive, so why not me? Seriously though, I wish I had realized that people were charging a lot more selling the same thing I was, and it was a lower quality service. I wish I would have given myself a lot more grace early on.

— Michelle Tresemer, *Co-Founder, Foundations First Marketing*

You Are the CFO of Your Business

The first step to effectively managing your finances is to comfortably step into your role as the Chief Financial Officer (CFO) of your business. You'll need to bring together the right team to support you. This team may include an accountant, a bookkeeper, a financial advisor, and possibly a lawyer.

Your accountant will advise you on business strategies, as well as tax planning and filing. Your financial advisor will work with you on overall financial and investment planning. Your bookkeeper will support you in managing the day-to-day tracking of your financial transactions and will also help you with filing taxes. You may work with a lawyer to review your contracts or to incorporate your business if you decide to take that route.

You can manage many of the financial functions yourself but remember to consider the best use of your time and zone of genius. I hired a bookkeeper in my fourth year of business, and I wish I had done it sooner. It freed up so much time and reassured me that everything was in proper order.

ENTREPRENEUR INSIGHT

The Top Three Numbers Every Business Owner Should Understand

One of the top questions I'm asked is "What are the most important numbers I should track in my business?" My answer is always: Sales, Net Profit, and Cash. These are the numbers that you should get in the habit of regularly reviewing.

Realistically, all numbers are important and work together to tell the real story. However, there are three numbers I always look at first if I'm looking at a new client's books that quickly give me an idea of the business's viability.

While these three numbers I'm about to share with you are important individually, each one is not an indicator of success on its own. Look at them together as part of a bigger picture.

Sales: Not to be confused with profit, sales (or revenue) is the money generated from selling your products or services before any costs are deducted. It is the first indicator of a business's viability, since without sales, you don't have a business! As important as sales are, however, they are not a measure of success on their own—there are other factors that should be considered in determining the success of a business.

Net Profit: Regardless of your sales, you need to ensure that your business is profitable. Net profit is your revenue, less any expenses incurred to generate your products/services and to run your business. When we focus on profit, we're able to see what we have left to pay ourselves (if we haven't yet), or more importantly, what we have left to reinvest back into our business. Consistent profit means you have a strong business model and are retaining funds that could be reinvested.

Cash: Cash is the tangible, hold in your hand indicator of how well a business is doing. Revenue and profit can sometimes be misleading in that they can often be inflated. For example, when you invoice your customers, your revenue is recorded but you won't always see the cash right away. A company's ability to retain cash is a strong indicator of good money management. Without cash, you can't pay your bills, or worse, yourself. A good cash balance also provides a strong safety net to cover unforeseen/ emergency expenses. Keeping an eye on your cash balance regularly and implementing cash management practices (like setting payment terms for your invoices) is extremely valuable.

— Jennifer Kapedani, *CPA*

Don't Let Expenses Slip through the Cracks

When you hear the terms "tax write-off" or "deductions," these are just alternate terms for business expenses. Any expense you incur in your business immediately offsets your revenue, which ultimately reduces your taxable income, which means you will pay less taxes.

This makes having a good bookkeeping system critical because the best way to ensure you're paying the least amount of tax is to make sure you're capturing every single business expense.

Create a Tracking System

You'll need a system to track your various invoices, receipts, and expenses. It can be as simple as using an Excel spreadsheet, or you can use a more complex financial software like Freshbooks or Quickbooks.

You will also need to develop a system for keeping all your receipts organized, either in hard copy or digitally. If you're using an app like FreshBooks or QuickBooks, you can scan all your receipts into the app. There are also applications like Hubdoc and Dext that allow you to capture and store receipts and other documents in one central repository with ease.

Alternatively, you can take pictures of your receipts and organize them into online folders by month. Also, set up folders to save copies of your invoices and monthly bank and credit card statements.

Sort and Separate Your Finances

I've heard horror stories of entrepreneurs who have comingled their business finances with their personal accounts. Often, this mistake can lead to a bookkeeping nightmare, or coming up short when taxes are due.

Set up a separate bank account and apply for a separate credit card, specifically for your business. When you first start your business, you may not qualify for a business credit card, so you can start with a personal card and apply for a business card down the road.

Set Aside Tax Money

In the corporate world, taxes were deducted from your paycheque by your employer. As a business owner, you earn revenue when you make sales in your business and a certain portion of that money will have to be paid in taxes. Depending on the requirements in your jurisdiction, you may be required to pay taxes monthly, quarterly, annually, or in installments.

Regardless of your schedule, it's a good idea to set up a separate account to put the approximate amount you will owe for taxes aside each month. Doing this will help make sure that when tax time comes, you don't end up short or accidentally use that money to make purchases.

Make a Date with Your Finances

It's easy to lose control of managing your finances, especially if it's not your favourite area of the business to manage, or if you hold the belief that you're not good with money. For many, it always seems to be the last thing you get to as piles of receipts form on your desk.

Make a one-hour date with yourself every week to focus on financial management. I have a weekly block in my calendar called "Money Mondays." Use this time to scan your receipts, create invoices, review your overall financial picture, and deal with any outstanding financial tasks.

If you're resistant to the idea of a weekly review, try to pair it with something you enjoy. Put on some good background music, maybe light a candle, or pour your favourite cocktail. Whatever it takes to make the experience feel more enjoyable for you, do it!

What are your key takeaways from this chapter?

What new ideas will you commit to trying or implementing in your business?

PART 4

Create Good Habits for Communicating and Connecting

MARKETING AND SALES ARE CRUCIAL TO growing your business. In this section, I am going to share some overarching ideas and approaches related to how you communicate and connect with the marketplace. When you boil it down, marketing and sales are simply acts of communicating and connecting.

We will start by talking about getting inside the mind of your client. From there, you can gather insights that will allow you to create effective content that connects with them. We will then talk about some mindset shifts related to marketing. We will also talk about ways to get more comfortable stepping into the spotlight as the face of your business.

And lastly, we will finish by discussing the value of your network and ways to stay connected. This section also includes some advice and tips from content creation experts.

Chapter 17

Get Inside the Mind of Your Client

TO EFFECTIVELY COMMUNICATE AND CONNECT with potential clients, you first need to develop a deep understanding of who you are serving. You need to get inside your client's mind by developing your ideal client profile (also commonly referred to as your "customer avatar" or "buyer's persona") to communicate in a meaningful way. In this chapter, I will use the acronym *IC* to refer to your *ideal client*.

Your IC will be found at the intersection of your expertise in helping to solve a specific problem and a person who is willing to pay to have someone guide them to solve their problem. Here are a few questions to get the ball rolling on developing your IC profile.

The first six questions would apply to a business that offers its product or service to other businesses. The rest of the questions will apply to all types of businesses.

1. What type of business do they have?

2. What industry or markets do they serve?

3. What stage of business growth are they in?

4. Where are they geographically located?

5. What significant event has happened in their business or life that would trigger a need for your services?

6. What is their role or title?

7. How would you define their personality, values, and beliefs?

8. What are their aspirations and dreams for the future?

9. What are their pain points and what do they worry about?

10. What are they missing that could help them reach their goals?

11. Is their challenge significant enough for them to invest money to solve it?

Pick a name for your IC and visualize them in as much detail as possible. Imagine a day in their life and picture them going through a challenge. What does their decision-making process look like? Incorporate your answers to the questions into a summary or story about your IC. This profile will help you put yourself in their shoes.

I would like to note that just because someone falls outside of the profile you have created, it doesn't mean you can't work with them. Some of my clients resist doing this exercise because they think it will restrict who they can work with. There are exceptions to the rule, but being clear on your IC profile is helpful because it will become the foundation for all your communications.

Narrow Your Focus

After you have gone through the exercise above, I want to challenge you: Have you been narrow enough in defining your IC profile?

If you have the mindset that everyone is your potential client, no one will be your client. It can feel uncomfortable to be specific, but the less specific you are, the less you'll be able to create messaging that connects with your potential clients, choose the right activities to attract them, or use your budget effectively.

For example, if you're a business coach and you say that you market to "anyone who needs coaching services," it is very likely that you'll have a difficult time attracting clients because they do not clearly understand what you can do for *them* specifically to solve *their* problem. Or you may find yourself attracting the wrong kind of clients.

Instead, if you narrow it down to "coaching for executive professional women who are transitioning back into the workforce after an extended parental leave," you're more likely to attract the right kinds of clients through marketing communications that speak to the issues specific to this type of client. You can also choose visuals to use in your branding that your IC will recognize themselves in.

This will help you narrow your market and provide products or services that align with your focus and skills.

ENTREPRENEUR INSIGHT

Get clear on what you offer and say NO to everything that isn't what you want to offer. My biggest failures in business came from when I took on projects for the money and not because they aligned with my skills.

— Lisa Wilson, *Human Resource Cultural Consultant and Leadership Coach, LMW Consultation*

In my case, there are many marketing consultants, but I differentiate myself by focusing specifically on providing marketing strategies and planning for service-based businesses that do not have in-house marketing expertise. I position myself as the "Marie Kondo of marketing." Marie Kondo is the famous professional organizer who sold millions of books sharing her formula for tidying up your home. I sell myself as bringing the same systematic and orderly approach to marketing: I help business owners get clear, organized, and into action to grow a thriving business.

ENTREPRENEUR INSIGHT

Starting your own business and persisting year after year is the most glorious, challenging, alive, university-of-life personal development process that ever existed. One of the things I learned early on was "I can help everyone" is not a marketing strategy. Pick a specific problem to solve. Pick a niche demographic to serve and go deep.

— Kira Callahan, *Founder and President, Conversation Gym*

Dig Deep to Find the Gold

To validate your profile and develop a deeper understanding of your ideal client, I suggest doing some additional research. As Jodie's story shows, it can be detrimental to make assumptions.

ENTREPRENEUR INSIGHT

Never Assume Your Client's Needs

Today, I am the owner of Clean Kiss Inc. which creates natural skincare for women, but I've had several careers. I started in an HR role in the corporate world. Following the birth of my twins, I decided that I was ready for a career change, and I bought a franchise of a daycare. I built the business and eventually bought a second franchise that was also successful.

I then saw the need for after-school care in the market and decided to launch a third business to cater to this market. Given that I was successful in the daycare market, and I was providing a similar offering, I made some assumptions that would prove to be detrimental to the business.

I assumed that my customers would want a well-rounded program that would offer a variety of activities including things like dance, yoga, and karate. To me, it seemed like the best of both worlds in providing an after-school solution and access to activities that parents would otherwise be paying for and taking their kids to separately. We even picked the school-agers up in a private bus from their respective schools and brought them to our facility, fed them a snack, helped them with their homework, and did sports with them until parents could pick them up by 6 pm. It seemed like the perfect business model!

Once I launched the business, I realized that parents weren't interested in having access to these types of programs in our type of generalized setting. If they were going to provide an opportunity for their child to participate in dance, they wanted to put them into the "right" dance studio to help them excel or the most highly rated karate dojo. Parents wanted a specialized opportunity for their kids, not a general place where they could learn something different every day.

I didn't get the enrollment I anticipated after heavily investing in the business for more than eighteen months. We ultimately had to close the business and took a significant financial loss.

Lesson learned for me: Never assume you know what your client needs. Take the time to do the research. Just because you are successful in one business model, it may not be transferable to a different demographic market.

— Jodie Pappas, *Founder, Clean Kiss*

Through a combination of online research and interviews with people that meet your profile, you'll be able to further understand their needs and capture language that you can reflect back to them when developing content. Using language that your customers naturally use is gold as it connects in a very direct way.

Conducting information-gathering interviews can also open the door for opportunities. To download a guide on how to research your ideal client and conduct client interviews, visit www.goodtogrowmarketing.ca/bookresources.

Developing an understanding of your client isn't a one-and-done exercise, but one you should come back to on a regular basis. Create a habit of continually asking questions of your potential clients to stay clear on what matters most to them. With this understanding, you'll be able to continue to find ways to develop offerings that serve their needs.

REFLECTIONS

What are your key takeaways from this chapter?

What new ideas will you commit to trying or implementing in your business?

Chapter 18

Communicate in a Way that Connects

REMEMBER HOW I MENTIONED THAT SHORTLY after resigning from my corporate job, I received an invitation to have lunch with a potential client? I recall preparing for the meeting and making a list of all the things I could share to convince him that I was, in fact, a marketing expert. I was concerned about proving my expertise and worth to him.

Make It about Them, Not You

When we sat down, I was running through the list in my head. After some small talk and getting to know each other, we started to talk about his business. As he shared some of his challenges, I naturally started to ask questions and offer insights and ideas. Something clicked when I realized that the lunch was not about me selling myself; he already assumed I had expertise, given that I was referred by someone he trusted. He wanted to know how I could help his business. That is what mattered to him.

It may sound obvious, but many new entrepreneurs fall into the trap of focusing on the features of their product or service or trying to prove their expertise. They don't realize that what the potential client really wants to know is how you can help them solve a problem they have. Shift your mindset from proving yourself to communicating the transformation you will help them experience.

Talk about Transformation

Regardless of the communication medium, whether it be copy on your website or a conversation, stay focused on sharing the benefits of what you offer and the outcome or transformation it will create.

People buy transformation. They are not buying the service or product you offer; rather, they are buying the outcome it will provide them with. It is important to be sure that you are communicating the *transformation*—how you get them from Point A to Point B. If they are buying an online workout system, they are not buying the videos or diet plan; they are buying the lean and healthy body they want to see in the mirror. They are buying the aspirational promise of going from tired and unhealthy to energized and fit.

If you focus on your product or service, you may communicate like this: "We have studied people's body types and created over eighty daily workouts. You'll get a diet plan included for no charge."

If you focus on their transformation, you may communicate more like this: "Are you tired of struggling to get up in the morning? Are you frustrated at how easily you lose your breath playing soccer with your kids? Do you avoid looking in mirrors? Get ready to feel lean, fit, and good about yourself. We've got the solution for you!"

That is why testimonials are such an effective marketing tool. Testimonials provide examples of the results someone else has achieved using your product or service. They help your potential client see how someone else had the same problem and overcame it with your help. Testimonials show how the client's life is better because they chose to work with your business.

Be the Guide, Not the Hero

How you communicate the transformation is important. Put the focus of your communications on the customer, not on your business or brand. A fun game is to click on a website and count how many times a business uses the word "we" vs. "you." You'll be shocked! A better approach is to speak directly to the customer by using more "you" statements.

Building a StoryBrand: Clarify Your Message So Customers Will Listen by Donald Miller is a great book that offers a simple approach to effectively communicating in a way that connects with potential clients and customers. The book's central premise is that in all your communications, the customer (not your business) should be the hero of the story.

The book takes you through the storytelling framework of a hero's journey. It is the story arc you see played out across everything from classic novels to Hollywood blockbusters: A character has a problem. They meet a guide that gives them a plan to overcome their challenge and inspires them to act. The character follows the instructions of the guide to achieve their desired outcome.

In using this framework, you position yourself as the guide that helps your client solve their problem, rather than being the hero who saves them. For example, if you are a consultant, rather than talking about how you have all the answers to solve your customer's problem, you demonstrate your credibility in a way that makes them trust you to guide them through their transformation.

Keep It Simple

Something funny often happens when I meet with a potential client. To prepare for the meeting, I look at their website and marketing materials to get a sense of who they are and what they offer.

When we meet and I ask them to tell me about their business, in many cases, there is a disconnect between what I've reviewed beforehand and what they tell me. In trying to create content they think is appropriate for "marketing communications" they end up creating content that doesn't reflect the essence of the business, or that is overly verbose or complicated.

Always keep your copy succinct and simple. Even if you offer a technical solution, avoid creating content that is too long or complex. People's attention spans are short. Don't make them have to work to try to figure out what you are trying to say. Make a habit of keeping it simple.

Have a Clear and Consistent Presence

Your "brand" will be created by combining your logo and supporting visuals with the content that creates a look, feel, and tone for the business that helps you stand out from your competitors. As you begin to develop your business, consider the voice of your brand. You can think of your brand voice as the personality of your business that is expressed through the content you create, be it written, video, etc. It should be consistent across all touchpoints with a client, regardless of the medium.

What do you want to be known for? How do you want your customers to feel when interacting with your brand? These are important questions to ask yourself so that you build a brand with intention that reflects you and your business.

When you communicate in a clear and consistent voice, you will attract your ideal clients.

ENTREPRENEUR INSIGHT

Six Ways to Hone Your Brand Voice

Establishing a brand voice is a simple and powerful way to help customers feel who you are and what you stand for. Creating a distinct experience from their point of view sends an energy that influences how people will feel and think about your brand, which affects how they'll interact with it.

Name three to five emotions you want people to associate with your brand. Pass all your copywriting (and images) through this filter to assess how accurately your content is evoking those feelings.

Create a brand voice chart. Google has tons of examples. List your brand's Voice Traits/Characteristics, your description of the trait, then a column for Dos and Don'ts. For example, if your brand voice is funny, you might be good to make people laugh. You can clarify to say you want to use humour with care but don't want to be too goofy.

Refine your tone. Are you funny or serious? Formal or casual? Matter of fact or enthusiastic? Irreverent or respectful? The more clearly you establish these boundaries, the easier you'll create or delegate copywriting.

Think like a big brand. The most successful convey their voice clearly and simply. Follow the leaders and practice, practice, practice.

Don't assume your brand voice is *your* voice. Unless you're building your personal brand, your brand voice may be different from your own voice.

Keep everything simple. You've got about three seconds to make an impression. This isn't pressure to be perfect, it's permission to let go of complexity and to see every opportunity as a chance for continuous learning and improvement.

— Trish Snyder, *Founder and President, Upwordly Content*

What are your key takeaways from this chapter?

What new ideas will you commit to trying or implementing in your business?

Chapter 19

Be of Service and Provide Value

"MARKETING" AND "SALES" CAN BE SCARY words for some business owners. There are often limiting beliefs connected to this area of business, and my hope is to offer you a different perspective. If you have a perception that marketing and selling is hard and that you don't like doing it, or that you are not good at it—it won't happen or you won't be effective. If you're going to build a business, you need to market. No business can exist without marketing.

Before you start thinking about your marketing tactics, I suggest reflecting on how you feel about marketing and do a mindset reframe if needed.

Reframe Your Idea of Marketing

When you think of marketing or selling, is it something you dread and avoid, or is it something you love that feels light and easy?

If you're in the first camp, it could be because of your perception of marketing. You might associate marketing or selling with trying to push something at someone or trying to convince them they need to buy something. This could be based on an experience you've had or how someone has tried to sell something to you.

What if, instead of thinking of it as marketing or selling, you take those words out of your vocabulary and think of it as client attraction?

Reframe it: think of it as helping, serving, or providing value. Your ideal client has a problem, and you exist to help them resolve it. Your ideal client already exists. Their problem already exists. Your job is to put your authentic self out there to connect with them. The people who resonate with what you are sharing will be attracted to working with you.

Whatever way you need to reframe it, embrace the idea of marketing and sales in a way that feels good and is right for you.

Help People Get to Know, Like, and Trust You

People want to work with people or brands they know, like, and trust. The goal of your initial and ongoing marketing efforts is to move people from not knowing anything about you or your business, to considering working with you, to signing on as a customer or client.

One of the best ways to do this is to regularly produce content that will be of service and offer value to your potential clients. You can create content in various forms including articles, blogs, videos, and downloadable resources. Sharing content regularly and often will keep your business top-of-mind and help you to establish your credibility. I suggest starting with whichever method of delivery (e.g., blog, short videos, LinkedIn posts) you feel most comfortable working with, and then branching out to others.

If you are not sure where to begin, make a list of all the questions your potential customers may ask and create content to answer those questions. Create a mix of educational, instructional, and inspirational content, and produce it in different mediums.

Content can be shared through your social media platforms or a blog on your website. Some content can be developed into a "lead magnet," meaning that someone provides their email address to access the content. A content marketing strategy helps build your email list, which allows you to nurture relationships with potential clients over time through continued connection. Content used in one format or on one platform can also be repurposed, so it is leveraged to maximize your efforts.

If writing is not your strength, a trick for easily creating written content is to voice record yourself talking about a subject or answering a question. Then, transcribe the recording through an affordable transcription service like Rev and edit the transcription into a final format.

You can also share your expertise and value by offering complimentary webinars or speaking at in-person or online events.

ENTREPRENEUR INSIGHT

Consistency Is Key

Consistency is so important. It takes years to get a following and get that momentum going. Really dial into what you want to be known for and then publish about it daily. I wish I would have started that years ago. But of course, imposter syndrome creeps in.

You don't have to be the expert right away, but you can initiate the questions. You can be the one who starts the conversations! Post with humility and an openness to learn and people will know, like, and trust you.

— Michelle Tresemer, *Co-Founder, Foundations First Marketing*

REFLECTIONS

What are your key takeaways from this chapter?

What new ideas will you commit to trying or implementing in your business?

Chapter 20

It's Your Time to Shine

FOR MOST OF MY CAREER, I WAS THE ONE helping someone else create the presentation or the video for the social media post. I lived behind the scenes, creating someone else's brand, and helping them connect with potential clients. Making the shift to becoming more visible as a business owner was a big adjustment for me. This is an area that I continuously work on as the vision for my business expands.

Shout from the Rooftops

You can't build a business while hiding under a rock.

You are the chief evangelist for your business, and you need to take advantage of every opportunity you have to shout about your business from the rooftops.

Many new entrepreneurs make the mistake of thinking that people know what they are up to. They may have shared a post or two about launching their business and then they go silent for fear of annoying their network. Or perhaps they share only with their professional network as they think they are sharing a business communication.

People are busy and they will miss many of your communications, so it's important that you communicate more than you think you have to. It takes the average person seeing the same message seven to twelve times before it even registers, and sometimes even more with the noise and distractions of social media.

ENTREPRENEUR INSIGHT

I didn't market my business at the beginning because I was afraid of what people would think and fear of looking like I was selling.

I felt there was a stigma associated with sales because I feared people would think I was not actually interested in them and their business. I have learned that you can be both selling AND genuinely interested in a person's business, and that's okay!

— Samara Starkman, *Managing Partner and Co-Founder at INQ IQ Consulting, Partner at INQ Law*

Don't worry about overdoing it. Keep showing up. Keep sharing. Keep connecting.

Come Out from behind the Curtain

In many traditional employment roles, your work is internally focused, so you don't need to be externally visible. When you step into entrepreneurship as the leader of your own business, you become the face of that business. You need to step into the spotlight. This can be a very uncomfortable transition that, to the detriment of their businesses, many entrepreneurs avoid making.

Like many people, I've always been self-conscious of how I look in photos and on camera. I pick apart images of myself and focus on how I don't like how my body or hair looks, or how my voice sounds. I've also been concerned about coming across confidently when I'm communicating my ideas.

Some of the best advice I ever received was to focus on the message I was delivering and how it could be of service, instead of thinking about myself and how I was delivering the message. By focusing on the person you are helping, your mind lets go of its focus on yourself.

Do whatever you need to do to feel more comfortable. Make time for it. Do the things that make you feel your best regularly and treat them with the same level of importance you would any other business activity. If working out makes you feel more confident, make time for it. If getting your nails done makes you feel like a million bucks, do it. As vain as it may sound, something as simple as a haircut or a new blouse can give you the boost you need to step into your new role as the face of your business.

You also need to be honest with yourself about the areas you need to work on to become more confident in showing up as the leader of your business. If there are areas you feel uncomfortable with, invest in the support you need to develop your skills. That may mean investing in an online program to learn how to go live on Instagram, or a public speaking coach that can teach you to become more comfortable giving presentations.

Do whatever you need to do so you can show up and shine.

Be Unapologetically You

The only person you can ever be is you. No more trying to fit into the employee or corporate persona that made you feel like a square peg squeezing yourself into a round hole.

Of course, you need to be professional to gain trust, but the more you can show up as your true self, the more comfortable you'll feel in putting yourself out there. When you reach this level of comfort and confidence, more people will connect with you because they will feel your authenticity.

There are no rules. Are you a natural storyteller? Tell stories. Do you have something in your life that you are passionate about? Show your enthusiasm. Are you the woman that blows away your potential clients with your wisdom AND rocks a leather jacket? Own it.

Smile for the Camera

Video is a powerful tool when you're working to establish trust. Through video, people can see you and experience how you communicate. It builds an emotional connection with potential clients, shares your message, and establishes authority.

Social media platforms also favour showing video content, making it a great marketing tool. If you don't have experience with making videos, that's okay. You can take small steps to become more comfortable. You can start by using a video messaging app like Marco Polo to share messages daily with a friend. This will help you get more comfortable with seeing yourself while being recorded.

It comes down to practising in order to build your confidence and embracing the suck as you go. A good way to push yourself is to create a habit of going live or sharing a video on a certain day of the week. By having a scheduled day, you train your mind to step into video mode and it becomes an automatic thing you do.

For example, a coach I follow goes live every Wednesday in her Facebook group at noon. This habit allows her to pre-schedule her time and topics, and consistently show up for her audience.

As a follower, I know when I can expect to hear from her and look forward to her videos.

ENTREPRENEUR INSIGHT

Getting Comfortable with the Camera

Making use of video is becoming increasingly important. The world has changed and we're not going back to the way it was. Video has become a huge part of how we communicate, but many people still shy away from the idea of creating video content. If you're just getting started, here are a few tips:

Personify the lens. Talking to a camera lens, an intimate object, can feel strange and daunting. You can trick your brain by "personifying" the lens to make yourself feel more comfortable. Think about the lens as being a person you are talking to, ideally someone you are comfortable with. Pretend you are having a conversation with that one person and tell them a story.

Use the right messaging formula. One big mistake I see people make, whether it is live or recorded video, is they begin by saying, "Hi everybody…" I immediately feel disconnected because I'm now just one in a sea of people that this person is talking to. A better approach is to start with an opening that will engage, like a bold statement, a statistic, or a thought-provoking question. Then introduce yourself and say, "I would like to share with you…" and move into educating your audience.

When you're starting, speak about your subject matter expertise and become known as an authority. That has nothing to do with promoting or selling your services. It is a mistake to be too promotional right out of the gate when you haven't built an audience yet. People can be turned off and never come back. Focus instead on being of service and building your authority.

— Sheryl Plouffe, *Owner, Sheryl Plouffe Media Inc.*

REFLECTIONS

What are your key takeaways from this chapter?

What new ideas will you commit to trying or implementing in your business?

Chapter 21

Work Your Network

DON'T UNDERESTIMATE THE VALUE OF HAVING conversations with people in your network. These conversations can spark word-of-mouth referrals that will be the most valuable source of business, especially in your early days. You never know who in your network is going to connect you to someone who could be a potential client. Former colleagues, friends, family, and parents of children your kids play sports with all make up your network.

Remember the story I told earlier about the first meeting I took when starting my business? If I had not shared the news of my business with a former colleague, he would not have thought of me when one of his clients needed help with marketing. That company became my first client!

One business owner I interviewed shared the following: "I have not spent a penny on advertising. Not even on Google or Facebook ads. I rely on word-of-mouth and relationship-building. This might not be the right path for every business, but I like to share this fact because I feel that many start-ups get bamboozled into large marketing spends needlessly."

BUSINESS INSIGHT

The Fifty Cups of Coffee Project

When I was leaving the corporate world, I took part in an activity that proved to be a hugely valuable exercise and taught me a lesson about the power of leveraging your network and connections.

When I resigned, I gave three weeks' notice and decided to make the most of that time to connect with people in my network. My goal was to learn everything I could that might help me forge my new path.

I made a list of fifty people who fell into three categories: those who had left the corporate world to start their own business; leaders of companies who could give me insights into their needs; and people who could be potential referral partners or suppliers. I called it my "Fifty cups of coffee project."

I reached out to each contact by email or through LinkedIn and asked for thirty minutes of their time. I told them I was leaving my corporate role and planning to create some form of consulting business, and that I would like to ask them some questions.

I managed to have coffee (yes, it was a lot of caffeine!), lunch, or phone calls with almost everyone on my list, and it was one of the most valuable things I did early on. I received a tremendous amount of great advice and was also introduced to even more people and resources. Down the road, some of those contacts became my most trusted vendors and referral sources.

This initial research also affirmed my hypothesis that there was a need for my business in the market. While I still didn't know exactly what my offering would look like, I had the first glimpse into the needs of my potential target market.

Stay top-of-mind with your network by regularly sharing content on social media, having conversations, and proactively reaching out to people in your network and beyond to build relationships. Make a point of getting out from behind your desk to attend in-person networking events whenever possible. Interacting with people face-to-face is the easiest way to develop relationships and establish trust.

BUSINESS INSIGHT

Leverage LinkedIn

LinkedIn is the world's largest professional network. It can be used to represent your personal brand and business, strategically build your network, and stay top-of-mind with referral sources and potential clients.

Your LinkedIn profile page is one of the first things to appear when someone searches your name, so it is worth investing the time to develop a solid profile. Be sure to use a professional photo and write a summary that explains how you help your clients. Also, ask key people in your network to write recommendations to enhance your credibility. Make sure your recommendations reference strengths and skill sets related to your new business. I have a framework I advise my clients to use when reaching out for recommendations that makes their request more likely to be fulfilled. You can download a copy at:

www.goodtogrowmarketing.ca/bookresources

Leave Everyone with an Impression of Increase

I've learned the importance of taking time to get to know people and fostering relationships. Never underestimate the value of relationships, and treat them accordingly. Assuming you have the right skill set to help solve someone's problem, at the end of the day, people work with people. You can have the fanciest branding, but it's doing the little things that other people don't take the time and effort to do that will make you stand out.

In *The Science of Getting Rich* by Wallace D. Wattles, the author says that we should leave everyone with the "impression of increase." This is the idea of leaving everyone you meet feeling better than before they met you. Developing this as a simple habit can make a massive impact.

Over ninety percent of my business has come from referrals. I believe that it is not only because of the service I provide, but because of the time I invest in building relationships and finding ways to leave people with an impression of increase.

That may mean sending a hand-written thank-you note or surprising them with a small gift. On one occasion, I sourced a dime from a specific year on eBay to give to a client as a gift to mark the anniversary of his business. We had shared a story connected to dimes, so the gift had a very specific meaning and touched him dearly.

Support and Be Supported by Strategic Partners

Always be thinking of potential alliances that would be beneficial to both parties. Depending on the type of business, strategically aligning with other businesses that have similar ideal clients can be a good strategy. Compared with establishing relationships with cold customers, a warm introduction can go a long way. For example, I have developed relationships with several strategy consultants because they naturally identify the need for marketing support during their strategy assessments.

Being able to offer the clients of your strategic partners the expertise they need also helps increase the value that strategic partner can deliver for their clients. In some cases, the strategic partner may ask for a referral fee if you secure a client. Others are just happy to have someone to refer clients to that they know they can trust.

Connect, Connect, Connect

Remember this acronym *ABC*: Always Be Connecting.

Keep this idea—*ABC*—in the back of your mind whenever you are meeting someone. As you learn more about what they do and their challenges, be thinking about who in your network you could connect them to. Of course, these connections need to be made in a sincere way. Offer to make an introduction and be sure you follow up to make it happen.

I focus on making these connections all the time, and people now think of me as someone who has a large network and is generous with facilitating connections. This is a great position to be in because it helps you create goodwill with your network and makes people in your network happy to reciprocate if you need an introduction in the future.

As a bonus, being a connector feels good! It puts good energy out into the universe that will come back to you in one way or another.

REFLECTIONS

What are your key takeaways from this chapter?

What new ideas will you commit to trying or implementing in your business?

Conclusion

"Our deepest fear is not that we are inadequate. Our deepest fear is that we are powerful beyond measure. It is our Light, not our Darkness, that most frightens us. We ask ourselves, who am I to be brilliant, gorgeous, talented, fabulous?

Actually, who are you not to be?"

— Marianne Williamson

WE'VE NOW COME TO THE END OF OUR JOURNEY together and I'm excited for you to start yours. With everything you've learned, you are *good to grow!*

I hope this book has inspired and empowered you with the knowledge and tools to thrive as an entrepreneur and create a life you love.

I want to remind you to enjoy the journey of building your business! Don't hang your happiness on reaching a certain milestone or revenue number.

Be happy in the experience of creating your vision. Celebrate yourself for each step you take. It feels so much better to fuel yourself with happiness and good-feeling thoughts than to bully yourself all the way to success.

A few important closing reminders:

Always remember you have something unique to offer to the world. You have a business that you are uniquely qualified to create because you are you.

Be clear on your vision, but also allow the journey to unfold as it's meant to, one step at a time.

Surround yourself with people who will support and inspire you.

Create the conditions necessary for you to thrive.

And finally, enjoy the beautiful life you're creating!

About the Author

LAURA VALVASORI is a Marketing Foundations Strategist & Mentor for Entrepreneurs, and the owner of *Good to Grow Marketing*.

Using her natural ability to distill, simplify, and organize, she's spent over twenty years helping businesses reach their goals and grow to new levels through practical, strategic marketing. She's been called the Marie Kondo of Marketing because she brings the same systematic and orderly approach to marketing to spark results for businesses as the famed professional organizer does for households.

Laura works with businesses varying from solo entrepreneurs and small businesses, to established private companies, across a variety of industries. By providing a combination of foundational marketing strategy consulting and business mentorship, she helps them get clear, organized, and into action so that they have the foundations to grow thriving businesses.

In recent years, Laura has mentored other entrepreneurs and launched *The Business Book Collective* as a way to give other like-minded entrepreneurs access to collective learning that helps spark new ideas and inspires them into action. She is a big believer in the power of community, masterminding, and collaboration as stepping stones to growth in business and in life.

Laura's desire to keep growing led her to writing her debut book, *Good to Grow*. Part memoir, part pocket mentor, the book is inspiring and empowering readers by guiding them through key areas to explore that are helping them grow into confident and thriving entrepreneurs. She wrote the book to share her experiences to help other entrepreneurs accelerate their learning, and hopefully save them some time, money, and a few tears.

By living the concepts shared in the book, Laura has created a successful business and beautiful life with her family. Laura runs her business from her "she-shed" in Oakville, Ontario, where she lives with her husband, two teenagers, and dog Remy. In the summer, you can find her on the water boating in Georgian Bay.

To learn more about working with Laura, visit:
www.goodtogrowmarketing.ca/

To access the free resources shared in this book, visit:
www.goodtogrowmarketing.ca/bookresources

Connect with Laura on her social platforms at:

Instagram: @goodtogrowmarketing
Facebook: www.facebook.com/goodtogrowmarketing
LinkedIn: www.linkedin.com/in/lauravalvasori

Works Cited and Resources

Books Cited

The following books have been referenced throughout *Good to Grow*. For your convenience, the list of books cited is provided as a reading list with links to purchase the books though Amazon if you visit: www.goodtogrowmarketing.ca/bookresources.

Clear, James. 2018. *Atomic Habits: An Easy & Proven Way to Build Good Habits & Break Bad Ones*. New York, NY: Avery Publishing.

Stanny, Barbara. 2014. *Sacred Success: A Course in Financial Miracles*. Dallas, TX: BenBella Books Inc.

Gerber, Michael E. 2001. *The E-Myth Revisited: Why Most Small Businesses Don't Work and What to Do about It*. New York, NY: HarperCollins.

Maltz, Maxwell. 1960. *Psycho-Cybernetics*. New York, NY: Simon & Schuster.

Rath, Tom. 2017. *Strengthsfinder 2.0 Discover Your CliftonStrengths*. New York, NY: Gallup Press.

Hogshead, Sally. 2016. *Fascinate: How to Make Your Brand Impossible to Resist*. New York, NY: Harper Business.

Fields, Jonathan. 2021. *Sparked: Discover Your Unique Imprint for Work that Makes You Come Alive.* Nashville, TN: HarperCollins Leadership.

Behrend, Genevieve. 2018. *Your Invisible Power.* Saint Paul, MN: Wilder Publications.

Duncan, Oonagh. 2020. *Healthy as F*ck: The Habits You Need to Get Lean, Stay Healthy, and Kick Ass at Life.* Naperville, IL: Sourcebooks Inc.

Proctor, Bob. 2021. *Change Your Paradigm, Change Your Life: Flip That Switch Now!* New York, NY: G & D Media.

Heriot, Drew (Director). 2006. *The Secret* [Film]. Prime Time Productions.

Wattles, Wallace D. 2018. *The Science of Getting Rich.* Saint Paul, MN: Wilder Publications.

Singer, Michael A. 2013. *The Untethered Soul: The Journey Beyond Yourself.* Oakland, CA: Noetic Books.

Pritchett, Price. 2012. *You²: A High Velocity Formula for Multiplying Your Personal Effectiveness in Quantum Leaps.* Dallas, TX: Pritchett.

Hill, Napoleon. 2010. *Think & Grow Rich.* Shippensburg, PA: Sound Wisdom.

Nightingale, Earl. 1956. *The Strangest Secret.* Wheeling, IL: Nightingale-McHugh Company.

Allen, Daniel. 2015. *Getting Things Done: The Art of Stress-Free Productivity.* London, UK: Little Brown Book Group.

Newport, Cal. 2016. *Deep Work: Rules for Focused Success in a Distracted World.* New York, NY: Grand Central Publishing.

de Mol, Eva, Jeff Pollack, and Violet T. Ho. 2018. "What Makes Entrepreneurs Burn Out." https://hbr.org/2018/04/what-makes-entrepreneurs-burn-out. Harvard Business Review.

Burchard, Brendon. 2017. *High Performance Habits: How Extraordinary People Become That Way*. Carlsbad, CA: Hay House.

Bernstein, Gabrielle. 2019. *Super Attractor: Methods for Manifesting a Life Beyond Your Wildest Dreams*. Carlsbad, CA: Hay House.

Michalowicz, Mike. 2018. *Clockwork: Design Your Business to Run Itself*. New York, NY: Portfolio.

Keller, Gary, and Jay Papasan. 2013. *The ONE Thing: The Surprisingly Simple Truth Behind Extraordinary Results*. Austin, TX: Bard Press.

Miller, Donald. 2017. *Building a StoryBrand: Clarify Your Message so Customers Will Listen*. Nashville, TN: Thomas Nelson Publishers.

Resources

Proctor Gallagher Institute: www.proctorgallagherinstitute.com

Catherine Farquharson, Mindset & Transformation Coach: www.mindsetcoaching.ca

Acknowledgements

I AM VERY FORTUNATE TO HAVE A STRONG NETWORK of people in my life who have supported me in the creation of this book. Thank you to my husband who has unwavering faith in me, and to my children who gave me the space to write on many early mornings.

Thank you to my mastermind sisters for acting as a sounding board, kicking my butt to keep writing, and cheerleading me to the finish line.

Thank you to Catherine Farquharson for guiding me on my mindset journey and for introducing me to the incredible women in your community who have supported my growth.

Thank you to each of my clients for placing your trust in me and giving me the experiences to share in this book. A special thanks to Walter Koppelaar for taking a chance on me.

Thank you to everyone who read early versions of this book and provided valuable insights. Your honest feedback and suggestions helped shape this book. I appreciate you taking the time out of your busy schedules to read. I know it is a big ask and I am truly grateful.

Thank you to all my family, friends (especially Alison Cruise, who read the evolving versions of this book many times!), and colleagues who have supported me in so many ways along my journey.

And finally, to anyone I've missed or who has supported me between the time of writing this book and having it published, thank you!

Contributors

Thank you to the over thirty women who shared their wisdom to contribute to this book. Their combined insights are woven throughout the content, and some are featured directly, including (listed in alphabetical order):

Cari Brunton, *Owner, Red Bucket Events*
www.redbucketevents.com

Kira Callahan, *Founder and President, Conversation Gym*
www.conversationgym.com

Laura D'Andrea, *Co-Owner, Smudge Allot Inc.*
www.smudgeallot.com

Valerie DuRoss, *Co-Founder, Crafted Communications*

Sharon Gilmour-Glover, *Co-Founder, Light Core Inc.*
www.light-core.com

Jennifer Kapedani, *CPA and Owner, Jennifer Kapedani*
www.jkcpa.ca

Jen Kelly, *Owner, New Initiatives Marketing*
www.newinitiativesmarketing.com

Cathy Landolt, *Founder, Blue Elephant Productions*
www.blue-elephant.ca

Cynthia Mason, *Founder and Managing Lawyer,*
Mason PC Trademarks
www.masonpc.com

Jodie Pappas, *Owner, Clean Kiss*
www.cleankisslifestyle.com

Saijal Patel, *TV Host, Strictly Money & Financial Wellness*
Educator & Consultant
www.saijelle.com

Sheryl Plouffe, *Sheryl Plouffe Media Inc.*
www.sherylplouffe.com

Trish Snyder, *Founder and President, Upwordly Content*
www.upwordlycontent.ca

Samara Starkman, *Managing Partner and*
Co-Founder at INQ IQ Consulting, Partner at INQ Law

Reina Takahashi, *Paper Artist*
www.reinasaur.com

Michelle Tresemer, *Co-Founder, Foundations First Marketing*
www.foundationsfirstmarketing.com

Teresa Vozza, *Executive Coach, Teresa Vozza Coaching*
www.teresavozza.ca

Lisa Wilson, *Human Resource Cultural Consultant and*
Leadership Coach, LMW Consultation
www.lmwcoaching.ca

Catherine Wright, *Sleep Coach, Educator and Speaker, Recoop*
www.recoop.care

With every donation, a voice will be given to
the creativity that lies within the hearts of
our children living with diverse challenges.

By making this difference, children that may
not have been given the opportunity to have their
Heart Heard will have the freedom to create
beautiful works of art and musical creations.

Donate by visiting

HeartstobeHeard.com

We thank you.

Manufactured by Amazon.ca
Acheson, AB

11412436R00131